The Prometheus Trilogy

Aeschylus'
Prometheus Trilogy

Prometheus Bound
translated by Henry David Thoreau

Fragments and descriptions of
Prometheus Unbound and
Prometheus the Fire Bearer

With an introduction by Nikolaus Wecklein

Edited with commentary by Charles Siegel

Second Edition

Omo Press

adolescentium alunt
senectutem oblectant

ISBN: 978-1-941667-22-4
Cover picture: Peter Paul Rubens: Prometheus with the Firebrand (1611-1612).
Some fragments were translated for this edition by Marissa Anne Henry.
Original material in this book is copyright © 2015, 2019 by Charles Siegel.

Contents

Preface 7

Introduction 11

Prometheus Bound 35

Prometheus Unbound 81

Prometheus the Fire Bearer 91

The Trilogy 97

Preface
by Charles Siegel

Classical tragedies were performed as a competition that lasted three days during the feast of the Great Dionysia. Three playwrights competed, with each presenting three tragedies and one satyr play in a performance that lasted for a day. Often, they wrote trilogies, with the three tragedies telling a continuous story. Only one complete trilogy survives, the Oresteia of Aeschylus, comprising *Agamemnon*, *Libation Bearers*, and *The Eumenides*. This trilogy as a whole is more powerful than the three plays would be individually.

There are also cases where we can reconstruct the trilogy based on fragments of plays that do not survive, on hints in the play that does survive, and on other accounts of the same myths. There are several reasons why it is particularly valuable to publish this reconstruction of the Prometheus trilogy of Aeschylus.

First, reconstructing the trilogy changes our view of its surviving play, *Prometheus Bound*. Read by itself, as it has been for centuries, *Prometheus Bound* seems to tell the story of Prometheus' heroic resistance to Zeus' tyranny. Reading the entire trilogy, we can see that the relation between Zeus and Prometheus is far more complex.

Second, we have a translation of *Prometheus Bound* by a great American author. Henry David Thoreau's translation was published in 1843 in *The Dial*, the most important magazine of the American Transcendentalist movement.

This edition is the first time Thoreau's translation has been made available to a general audience in book form.

Third, excellent work on reconstructing this trilogy has already been done by a series of classical scholars, ranging from the nineteenth-century German scholar N. Wecklein to the contemporary scholars Mark Griffith and Alan Sommerstein.

There has been a great deal of dispute among scholars about how the trilogy should be reconstructed. Most scholars have concluded that the plays should be in the same order as in this book: *Prometheus Bound*, *Prometheus Unbound*, and *Prometheus the Fire Bearer*. But there has been a wide range of theories, including the suggestion that there was no trilogy, and *Prometheus Bound* was written by another playwright as a response to Aeschylus' *Prometheus Unbound*. The two most authoritative editions both disagree with the order used in this book. Mark Griffith's edition put the plays in the order *Prometheus the Fire Bearer*, *Prometheus Bound*, *Prometheus Unbound*.[1] Alan Sommerstein's edition says that *Prometheus Bound* is followed by *Prometheus Unbound*, but *Prometheus the Fire Bearer* cannot possibly go either before or after these two plays.[2]

There is clearly uncertainty involved, but this edition gives a plausible interpretation of the fragments that puts the plays in the order *Prometheus Bound*, *Prometheus Unbound*, *Prometheus the Fire Bearer* and that creates a coherent and dramatically powerful trilogy.

This edition includes an abridged version of Wecklein's introduction to his book, which provides a thorough account

---

[1] Mark Griffith, *Aeschylus: Prometheus Bound: Cambridge Greek and Latin Classics* (Cambridge and New York, Cambridge University Press) 1983, p. 282.

[2] Aeschylus, *Fragments*, edited and translated by Alan H. Sommerstein (Cambridge, Mass, Harvard University Press, 2008), p. 212.

of the history of the Prometheus myth and of the issues involved in reconstructing the trilogy. Because this edition is aimed at the general reader, it includes only fragments that quote from the plays. There are several other fragments that refer to the plays but do not quote from them, which are available in Griffith's edition.

The Prometheus Satyr Play

Trilogies of Greek tragedy were accompanied by a satyr play, which presented comic action featuring a chorus of satyrs. The satyr play was related to the tragedies, reminding us that these plays were performed at the Dionysia, a festival honoring the god of wine and license.

Aeschylus wrote a satyr play about Prometheus, named *Prometheus the Fire Kindler*. Plutarch tells us that

> The Satyr, at his first sight of fire, wished to kiss and embrace it, but Prometheus said,
> "You, goat, will mourn your vanished beard."[3]

Yet most scholars agree that this satyr play was performed with the trilogy that included Aeschylus' *The Persians*, and that it is not connected with the Prometheus trilogy, so it is not included in this book. Nothing is known about the satyr play performed with the Prometheus trilogy.

The Author

From Hellenistic times until the nineteenth century, *Prometheus Bound* was attributed to Aeschylus, but his

---

[3] From Plutarch, "How to Profit by One's Enemies" Translation from Plutarch, *Moralia* translated by Frank Cole Babbitt (Harvard University Press, Loeb Classical Library, 1928) volume 2, pp. 8-9.

authorship is now in doubt because its simple prose style, its short choral lyrics, and the words it uses are different from the six other surviving plays by Aeschylus. In 1857, R. Westphal suggested that the play was originally written by Aeschylus but reworked by another author, and in 1911, A. Gercke was the first to suggest that the play was not written by Aeschylus at all. Mark Griffith wrote a book that describes the controversy at length.[4] He also summarizes the controversy briefly in his edition of *Prometheus Bound*, and he concludes, "With the limited evidence available to us for comparison (less than one-tenth of Aeschylus' *oeuvre*), we cannot hope for certainty one way or the other."[5]

If the Prometheus trilogy was by another playwright, then he deserves a place alongside the great classical tragedians, Aeschylus, Sophocles, and Euripides. *Prometheus Bound* has long been considered one of the greatest Greek tragedies and has had a powerful influence on western literature, inspiring poems by Goethe and Byron and a play by Shelly.

Whoever the author is, *Prometheus Bound* is clearly a great work of literature—and we will see that the Prometheus trilogy as a whole is even more powerful than this one play.

---

4 Mark Griffith, *The Authenticity of Prometheus Bound* (Cambridge and New York, Cambridge University Press) 1977.

5 Mark Griffith, *Aeschylus: Prometheus Bound*, p. 34.

Introduction
by N. Wecklein[6]

Earliest Origins of the Prometheus Myth

Fire is the celestial agency which aids man in all the arts of life. As man grows in independence, in self-consciousness, as he feels in himself the ability to guard against misfortune by his own prudence, he becomes aware of a distinct break with his past life. What formerly he expected from the grace of the gods, and sought to obtain through sacrifices, he now believes that he can get by his own skill. Accordingly this transition from barbarism to civilization comes to be associated with the idea of a Titan-like struggle on the part of men to make themselves equal to God — with the notion of a curtailment of divine privileges for the advantage of the human race, and of defiance and revolt against the gods.

Out of these conceptions, the story of Prometheus, in its

---

6 This introduction is an abridged version of the introduction of N. Wecklein, *The Prometheus Bound of Aeschylus and the Fragments of the Prometheus Unbound*, translated by F.D. Allen (Boston, Ginn and Company, 1891). Wecklein includes the text of the play and fragments in Greek and his commentary in German. Allen translated the German of the second edition of Wecklein's book, published in 1878. This introduction reprints Allen's translation, retaining the spelling and punctuation of the original, and making the original more readable by abridging it and adding more subheadings.

various shapes, has gradually grown. The origin of this myth is to be sought in the time when the Indo-European peoples still formed one community. Fire comes in two ways. Either it descends from the sky as a flash of lightning and kindles a tree or shrub, or it is obtained by friction. The first is the older way and furnishes the rudiments of the myth. In the ancient Hindu legend, Agni, the divine impersonation of fire, is brought down to mortals from the sky. A frequent surname of Agni is *Pramati* that is, 'Forethought,' 'Providence.'

But fire was obtained, in ancient times, by the twirling motion of a wooden rod bearing upon the centre of a wheel or disk of wood, — a method practised in India to the present day in kindling the pure sacrificial fire. The twirling stick or drill was called *pramanthas* (from *math-*, *manth-*, *mathami* 'turn,' 'twirl'); and this word is the ultimate source of the name Prometheus.

These two conceptions of the origin of fire became, in the course of time, more or less combined and fused. The fire-drill came to be identified with Agni Pramati; the fire-borer was metamorphosed into a provident fire-bringer, who kindled an inflammable shrub at the fire of the sky and brought it down to the earth. So arose the Greek notion of a 'Forethinker,' Prometheus, of vaguely defined nature, but thought of rather as superhuman than divine, who steals fire from the chariot of the Sun, from the hearth of Zeus, or from the forge of Hephaestus, brings it to men in a tinder-stalk, and so becomes the founder of human civilization.

In the Attic religious system, Prometheus appears as a simple god of civilization, in intimate union with Hephaestus and Athena. Just outside of Athens was the *Kolonos hippos,* a hill sacred to Poseidon, which furnished the potters' quarter of the city, the *Kerameikos*, with admirable clay for the famous and much-sought Attic vases. Between this hill and the city lay the Academy, the sacred grove of the hero Academus. Here Prometheus was worshipped in conjunction with Hephaestus and Athena. In the space dedicated to the goddess Athena stood an old statue of Prometheus, with an altar. At the entrance was a pedestal with a relief representing Prometheus and Hephaestus. Prometheus was here figured as the more prominent and older god, with a sceptre in his hand; Hephaestus as younger and less important. On the same pedestal a common altar of the two deities was represented. In honor of Prometheus the festival called *Prometheia* was annually celebrated, with a torch-race from the Academy to the city. The torches were lighted at the altar of Prometheus, and the runners endeavored to outstrip each other without extinguishing their torches.

This solemnity is the remnant of an exceedingly ancient religious observance—the Renewal of Fire. The idea of a difference between pure, celestial fire and fire which has been defiled by human use is common to the Indo-European nations; and this notion led to the custom of replacing, from time to time, the polluted fire in house and workshop by the pure element, in the belief that this would bring renewed prosperity.

How the torch-race arose from this usage, can best be seen from the following story, told by Plutarch in his life of Aristides, chapter 20. When the Greeks, after the battle of Plataea, consulted the Delphic oracle respecting the sacrifices they should make, the god gave directions that, as the fire in that region had been polluted by the barbarians, no sacrifices should be made until it had all been extinguished and fresh fire brought from the common hearth at Delphi. On this, the leaders of the Greeks ordered all fire throughout that country to be quenched, and the Plataean Euchidas proceeded to Delphi, promising to bring the new fire from the Delphic sanctuary with all possible despatch. He purified himself, sprinkled himself with holy water, and put a chaplet of laurel on his head. Taking the fire from the altar, he set out at full speed for Plataea, and arrived there the same day before sunset, having traversed a distance of a thousand stadia. He had only strength to greet his fellow-townsmen and give them the fire, when he fell to the ground and breathed his last.

It was thought needful, we see, that the transportation of the fire should be as rapid as possible, so that its original purity might be preserved, and a continuity, as it were, established between the altar at Delphi and the new hearth at Plataea. In like manner at Athens the pure fire was taken from the altar of Prometheus and borne with the utmost despatch into the city to the quarter of the smiths and the potters. It is clear that at Athens Prometheus was a fire-god who stood in a very intimate relation to the handicrafts of the place.

Prometheus in Hesiod

In the Hesiodic poetry (*Theogony* 535 ff., *Works and Days* 47 *ff.*) we find the myth of Prometheus detailed at length, but curiously interwoven with ethical ideas and overlaid with additions made with evident design. A naive, peasant-like conception of civilization here finds expression, as something which has led men into resistance to the divine will, and so has brought evil into the world by way of retribution. In the *Theogony* the story runs thus:

When gods and mortal men were divided at Mecone,[7] then the artful, crafty-souled Prometheus, son of the Titan Iapetus and of Clymene, brother of the sturdy Atlas, the

---

[7] That is, when, at the accession of Zeus to power, the separation of gods and men took place, and the patriarchal community in which the two races had lived together under Cronus had come to an end. [Wecklein's note]

high-souled Menoetius, and the blundering Epimetheus, sought, in the division of a sacrificial ox, to deceive the mind of Zeus. He laid on one side, as the portion of men, the flesh and the rich inner parts, wrapped them in the skin, and laid the ox's stomach upon them; on the other side he set apart for Zeus the white bones, artfully heaped up, and concealed by shining fat. Taken to task by Zeus for this unequal division, he smiled roguishly, and bade Zeus take his choice. Zeus perceived the trick, and foreboded evil in his heart to mortal men,—evil which was destined to be fulfilled. He raised with both hands the fat, and waxed mightily wroth as he beheld the white bones beneath. In penalty, fire was withheld from mankind.

But the son of Iapetus, friendly to man, outwitted Zeus, and stole the fire's far-flashing brightness in a hollow tinder-stalk. For this Zeus sent an evil on mankind. At his bidding, Hephaestus fashioned of clay a woman, whom Athena endowed with all charms. Then he gave to men the beautiful bane, and from her sprang the race of women, who dwell as a great plague among mortal men, like the drones of a bee-hive. But the kind-souled Prometheus, as a warning that Zeus's mind is not to be deceived, was bound to a pillar by chains riveted through its middle. Then Zeus sent an eagle which devoured Prometheus's imperishable liver; there grew each night as much as the bird had consumed by day. The eagle was slain by Heracles, and thus the son of Iapetus was delivered from his pain, not against Zeus's will, to the end that Heracles' fame should increase upon the broad earth.

According to the *Works and Days*, Zeus conceals the fire because Prometheus has deceived him, but Prometheus secretly purloins it again from Zeus. In retribution for this, Zeus sends to Epimetheus the woman Pandora, endowed by all the gods with manifold gifts. Epimetheus receives her against the express warnings of his brother, and knows not the evil till it is upon him. For till then the generations of men upon earth had lived free from pain and heavy sorrow, and free from deadly disease. But the woman lifted the lid from the jar, and all sicknesses and sorrows flew forth and spread over land and sea. Only Hope remained within, for Pandora at the behest of Zeus had closed the lid before she could escape.

These two narratives seek to explain how evil came into the world. The first conception, that increased material comfort brought with it luxury and its evil consequences, appears to be more primitive and simpler than the other idea, that misery came into the world through womankind. Both conceptions are united in the account of the *Works and Days*, in which Pandora is no longer ancestress of the human race, but an independent personage. Prometheus is conceived as the genius of humanity. The human race, by a crime against Deity (for Prometheus fancies himself wiser than Zeus) brings on itself divine retribution, and therewith all the pain and misery of life.

Prometheus in Aeschylus

Prometheus is the son of the goddess Themis,[8]—his father is nowhere mentioned. In the struggle between the Titans and Zeus he had at first sided with the Titans; afterwards— since he learned from his mother Themis that the victory would be decided, not by brute strength, but by craft and stratagem, and since the Titans rejected his counsels,— he forsook the losing cause, and ranged himself, with his

---

8 Themis was an ancient Titaness. The name means "divine law." Most myths say Themis is the daughter of Gaia, the ancient earth goddess, but Aeschylus has Prometheus identify Themis with Gaia: "Themis, and Gaia, of many names one form...."

mother, on the side of Zeus, to share in the fruits of victory. With his effective aid, Cronus and the Titans were hurled into the abyss of Tartarus. But in the adjustment and regulation of the new empire, a dispute arose between Zeus and Prometheus.

It was Zeus's wish to destroy the old race of mankind which had existed during the era of the Titans, and replace it by a new race adapted to the new order of things. But Prometheus came forward as the champion of the old generation of men, imbecile and insensate though they were. He awoke them to active exertion, he gave them fire stolen from the gods, he taught them all arts and handicrafts; in short, by developing in them thought and consciousness, he not only assured their existence, but made it nobler and happier.

But the day of license, of independent action, is past; every one has now his allotted post and his prescribed function. A universal regime, with Zeus at the head, has been established, to which the individual must conform, though conformity may seem, in contrast to the olden time, to involve suppression of personal freedom. So Prometheus's willful infringement of the new system, his revolt against the sovereign of the world, must needs be severely punished, — the more severely because Zeus's empire is new, and can be fortified only by prompt and vigorous measures against every act of insubordination.

Prometheus Bound

Cratos and Bia [Strength and Force], ministers of Zeus and personifications of his stern discipline, drag Prometheus to a wild region of Scythia, on the confines of the world; there Hephaestus nails him to a lofty cliff near the ocean. This severe punishment seems to Prometheus the height of ingratitude and cruelty on Zeus's part, — ingratitude toward one who has been his faithful ally in the stress of the conflict with the Titans, and cruelty toward a fellow-deity whose only offence lies in having done good to mankind. Such sufferings, borne with fortitude, may well awaken pity; and the daughters of Oceanus, compassionate natures, startled by the resounding blows of the hammer, approach and utter bitter complaints against the cruelty of the new sovereign of Olympus.

But Prometheus is not bound down to passive endurance. He has the means of active resistance, for he knows a secret, on the knowledge of which Zeus's future depends. He knows that Zeus will hereafter contemplate a marriage with Thetis, and that the son born from this union is destined to be mightier than his sire.[9] With the aid of this secret, Prometheus thinks to take signal vengeance on his tormentor. Zeus must humble himself, or be hurled from his throne, like Cronus before him, and Uranus before Cronus. In the assurance that a day of reckoning will hereafter come, Prometheus receives with a scornful smile the offers of Oceanus, who now appears, ready to intercede with Zeus in the hope that by timely reconciliation and submission, Prometheus may be admitted to pardon. These prudent counsels come prematurely, the authority of their propounder is insufficient, and Prometheus is himself in too passionate a frame of mind. Confident that the right is on his side, he treats Oceanus as a compliant weakling, caring only for his own ease and safety. The offer of mediation fails of its intended effect; far from being moved to submission, Prometheus is only strengthened in his resistance.

From this sullen mood he is roused to violent passion by

---

9 Thetis was a sea nymph, one of fifty daughters of the ancient sea god Nereus. After Prometheus told Zeus the prophecy, Zeus married Thetis to Peleus, King of Aegina, and their son was Achilles, who was mightier than his father.

a visit of the frenzied Io,[10] the daughter of Inachus. Chosen by Zeus as his favorite, she is pursued by the jealous fury of Hera, driven from land to land and sea to sea, through the abodes of many horrible monsters. Although Prometheus knows, from the prophecies of his mother Themis, that Zeus is to bring Io's sufferings to a happy conclusion, and that from the progeny of Zeus and Io is to come his own deliverer, nevertheless passion stifles in him all sober thought; he sees in this act of Zeus nought but a wanton outrage, and his indignation and thirst for revenge pass all bounds. The measure of his guilt is full; he utters a speech of defiance and abuse, which Zeus can no longer overlook. Hermes, sent by Zeus, appears and demands with dire threats the revelation of the secret which Prometheus vaunts so loudly. The messenger is dismissed with insult and mockery, and his threats are now fulfilled. In the midst of thunder, lightning, and a tumult of the elements, Prometheus, together with the rock to which he is bound, is hurled into the abysses of the earth, and his insolent speech is stifled. So ends the *Prometheus Bound*.

Prometheus Unbound

Many ages elapse, and at length the rock to which Prometheus is fastened emerges on the heights of Caucasus. The sullen wrath of the Titan still remains. In punishment, an eagle is sent every third day to devour his liver (the seat of passion); the liver, however, immediately grows again. Prometheus had formerly boasted that as an immortal he could not be killed by Zeus; now he longs for death (see Fragment III). Made pliant by suffering, he is now less

---

10 Io was loved by Zeus and changed by the jealous Hera into a cow, guarded by hundred-eyed Argus. When Argus was killed, she was chased through the world by a gadfly. She recovered her own form in Egypt. She was an ancestor of Heracles.

averse to compromise than when he rejected the offer of Oceanus. Zeus, however, has meanwhile released the Titans from Tartarus and become reconciled with Cronus. The curse of Cronus no longer rests upon him, and the guilt is removed which formerly attached to his dynasty and endangered its continuance. The Titans themselves come to visit Prometheus (Fragment I) and give him tokens of reconciliation and peace. Zeus of his own accord has set them free; his dominion is assured; there is no longer fear of any insurrection. Now without detraction from his dignity he can offer the hand of reconciliation to Prometheus, whose defiant spirit is at last broken. Zeus makes one condition — the revelation of the secret; but this is now a matter of mere form, because the reconciliation between Zeus and Cronus has done away with all actual danger to Zeus. So a compact is made. Prometheus divulges the secret, upon a promise from Zeus that he shall be freed from his fetters.[11]

Prometheus has carried his point; Zeus, in appearance, has made the first concession. But this concession is after all a formal one, and involves no humiliation of Zeus; the unbiased observer cannot but feel the character of Zeus to be the higher and nobler.

In this way the first step towards a reconciliation is made. The part of mediator was taken, it would seem, by Gaea, the mother of the Titans. As in the *Prometheus Bound* an unsuccessful attempt at mediation intensifies the bitterness of Prometheus towards Zeus, so now a successful attempt heralds the return of friendlier feeling. In like manner, as the height of Prometheus's fury was marked by the appearance of Io, so it is obviously suitable that Heracles, her descendant, should now complete the work of reconciliation. Heracles is sent by Zeus and slays the eagle

---

[11] Wecklein may be wrong about this, based on other versions of this myth. See the section below entitled "One Missing Detail."

(see Fragments V and VI[12]). Nevertheless this is not done without an expiatory offering. The centaur Chiron had been accidentally wounded by Heracles with a poisoned arrow, and the only possible deliverance from the agony of the incurable wound is in death. The undeserved sufferings of Chiron Heracles offers to Zeus as an offset for Prometheus's merited sufferings, and the voluntary death of the centaur (for Chiron is by nature immortal) is to atone for the guilt of the chained Titan.

By this act it is distinctly and solemnly proclaimed that Prometheus is in the wrong. Though formally the victor, he is in reality humiliated and brought to a tacit acknowledgment of guilt. All the circumstances show themselves now in a different light. How differently, for instance, appears the passion of Zeus for Io. From her is sprung Heracles, the benefactor of the human race, the pattern of heroic virtue. Heracles, as well as Io, has to undergo untold hardships before he enters into his rest in the abode of the blessed, and receives the blooming Hebe as his spouse. Prometheus describes to him his wanderings, much as he had described hers to Io, enumerating the dangers and toils which he must encounter on the journey to the Hesperides (Fragments VII-IX[13]). He advises him, among other things, not to endeavor himself to obtain the golden apples, but to send Atlas for them, taking meanwhile the burden of the sky upon his own shoulders.

Zeus therefore it is who ordains all things for good. Prometheus cannot but acknowledge this, and is obliged to admit that Oceanus's former advice was right, and to act accordingly. The acceptance of a vicarious punishment in atonement for his own guilt involves submission and

---

12 Fragments 9 and 10 in this edition.

13 Fragments 5 through 7 in this edition.

humiliation, and his repentance is finally sealed by his liberation from bonds. Probably this was performed not by Heracles, but by Hermes, at Zeus's command. By way of voluntary penance Prometheus places on his head a wreath of *agnus castus* (*lugos* in Greek), a sort of osier often used for fetters, and enjoins upon mankind, in whose behalf he had suffered, to wear this same wreath in remembrance of his bonds. To the penance and humiliation which he once thought to force on Zeus Prometheus himself submits.

Interpretations of Aeschylus' Plays

So long as the *Prometheus Bound* was considered by itself, as a single play, and its inner connexion with the *Prometheus Unbound* was disregarded, it was gravely misunderstood. The fact of Zeus's justice and rectitude, placed by the poet far in the background, was easily overlooked; Prometheus's specious pleas, loudly awakening our sympathy and interest, obscured the real and fundamental idea. It was believed that Aeschylus meant to depict in Zeus the cruel, passionate, arbitrary tyrant; in Prometheus, the pattern of a true friend of humanity. Or Prometheus was taken as a type of the human race in its struggle with the forces of nature, armed only with unshakable will and the consciousness of its lofty mission; and the central, ennobling idea of the play was thought to be the triumph of submission. Others, again, imagined that the main purpose of the drama was the glorification of Fate as the supreme, eternal power of the universe, presiding over the conflict of a great intellect with the will of a thankless tyrant, the conflict of humanity against the combined force of hostile gods and hostile nature — 'of great gigantic Fate, which lifts man up while it crushes him to earth.' Finally it was laid down that two conceptions of Zeus had to be distinguished in Aeschylus's plays, — the

Zeus of the current mythology and the Zeus of the poet's own ideal; and that in the Prometheus the imperfect Zeus of the popular legends was represented.

Welcker showed that the preserved play must be taken as part of a larger whole—a trilogy, and cannot be understood except in connexion with the rest of the trilogy. Aeschylus was a deeply religious man, and the belief, which pervades all his poetry, that Zeus is an eternal, righteous, all-powerful ruler of the universe, must surely have been dominant in this trilogy as elsewhere. If anything seems to contradict this belief, it must have had its explanation and justification in the composition of the whole work.

Aeschylus had before him a twofold conception of Prometheus. The Attic mythology presented him as a pure divinity of nature, as a benign and venerable object of worship. The rustic theology of Hesiod, according to which all civilization was opposed to the divine will, gave to Prometheus, as the representative of the human race, the character of an impious rebel, seeking the aggrandizement of mankind at the expense of the gods, and bringing on men heavy punishment from the gods. Aeschylus undertook to combine the two myths. At the outset he makes Prometheus an enemy of the gods, rebelling against their authority in a spirit of self-will and defiance, and disturbing the order of the universe, to the advantage of mankind, it is true, but against divine right. At the end, the same Prometheus appears as a deity of human culture, at peace with the other gods and much revered in his own province.

Several traits of the Hesiodic narrative Aeschylus found unsuited to his use. The fraud in the apportionment of the sacrificial ox and the punishment of mankind by the gift of woman were omitted, and so was the fiction of a brother Epimetheus. Altogether, Aeschylus could not rest satisfied with Hesiod's explanation of the origin of evil. He adopted the Hesiodic tradition of a succession of different ages and races of mankind, but he thought out a theory which refused to ascribe the source of evil to Zeus and the other gods, and sought to reconcile the imperfection of human nature with the perfection of Zeus's government. Zeus, — so Aeschylus imagined, — on his accession to power, had intended, as part of his wise and perfect reorganization of the universe, to replace the existing race of men, which had survived from early times and still led the stupid unreasoning life of those times, by a new and more perfect race, endowed with qualities like his own. He did not wish to destroy humanity from jealousy or hate, but only to destroy the present human race in the interest of the general good.

Prometheus, the short-sighted 'Forethinker' for the immediate and the individual, stepped forth in opposition to Zeus's far-reaching plan. He became the preserver of the existing human race, but at the same time the perpetuator of human imperfection, for all his services and benefits could not remove this imperfection. Furthermore, Prometheus's resistance has destroyed all claim of mankind on Zeus's beneficence. The old state of things remains; only Prometheus, who sought to remedy the deficiencies of men by interfering with the rights of the gods, is severely punished for his presumption and injustice.

The poet has set two views over against one another, — a calm, steady judgment and an unreasoning sentiment. On one side stands Zeus, the powerful far-seeing ruler, who punishes sin relentlessly and imparts 'wisdom through woe' (Aeschylus' *Agamemnon*, 177), whose eye is bent on the whole and not on details; on the other side Prometheus, passionate and proud, with a Titan's vehemence and impatience of control, doing good from unreasoning impulse, winning affection by his kind offices, but failing to meet the demands of a rational judgment. Prometheus is therefore a truly tragic character: he is great and lofty in his love for mankind, his daring deeds, and his fortitude in suffering; he arouses our sympathy and interest, but by his one-sided zeal and reckless acts he merits and receives reprobation.

The poet has depicted Prometheus's revolt with admirable skill. His spectators believed as firmly as himself in the wisdom and justice of Zeus; he neither could nor would deceive them by letting these qualities be for the moment obscured; his aim was to interest them in the plot and awaken their curiosity. The momentary illusion is justified on artistic grounds, for a revolt against the divine government can spring only from short-sightedness. Nothing but short-sightedness can make it appear as if Zeus hated and envied mankind, – Zeus, who sent his son Heracles to be a champion of humanity. Short-sightedness it is which makes Zeus's treatment of Io seem willful cruelty.

The inner history of the revolt, the thoughts and passions of the disputants, are not directly described, but according to ancient custom are allowed to show themselves in outward actions and the characters of the several personages. Prometheus's own attitude appears in the tone in which he speaks of his secret, and utters the hope that Zeus will be humbled (verses 167, 186, 520, 757, 907). In this way the dramatic effect of the play is enhanced.

The revolt is the subject of our drama. But an aimless action is no fit dramatic subject. A revolt without inner meaning, a mere bickering of one god with another, would produce no suspense, and would be simply an unpleasing spectacle, most of all to the religious-minded spectator. That tension of interest which is essential to a good tragedy, Aeschylus has produced by the introduction of a myth, which originally had no relation to the story of Prometheus. He used a story which we read in its older form in Pindar

(*Isthmian* vii, 60). Themis—so ran the legend—when Zeus and Poseidon wooed Thetis, had pronounced the decree of fate that the sea-goddess should bear a son mightier than his sire; should Zeus or Poseidon be united to her, this son would wield a weapon more powerful than thunderbolt or trident.

Aeschylus omitted the reference to Poseidon, made Prometheus participant in the fatal secret which properly belonged to Themis, and to this end made him a son of Themis instead of a son of Clymene. The knowledge of this secret (for that which originally was an incidental revelation had for dramatic purposes to be represented as a carefully guarded secret) the poet makes the turning-point of the whole plot. The continued enmity between Zeus and Prometheus, and their final reconciliation, both depend on it.

A danger threatening the sovereignty of Zeus,—this is the substance of the secret. This danger must have its cause. Now Zeus's sovereignty was universally believed to be everlasting; accordingly this cause must needs be a temporary one, which shall finally result in nothing. Such a cause the poet found in the downfall of Cronus and the conflict of duties which beset Zeus at that time. It was right that brute force should be deposed by the reign of intelligence; such is the law of the universe. In the struggle with the Titans, Zeus was in the right, and Themis herself, the representative of sacred law and eternal order, stood on his side in this struggle. As ruler of the universe, therefore, Zeus, in overthrowing the Titan dynasty, simply fulfilled his higher duty; but in his personal capacity be violated filial piety by laying forcible hands on his own father, and piety toward parents was one of the most sacred laws, for the maintenance of which the Erinyes kept strictest watch. In Aeschylus' *Eumenides* (641) the Erinyes themselves speak of this offence: 'He (Zeus) has himself thrown his aged sire Cronus into chains.' Zeus, then, was guilty, having sinned against the Fates and the Furies, and whoever is guilty must perish.

This guilt of Zeus was made by Aeschylus the cause of the impending danger to Zeus. Yet his was after all an innocent sin—more innocent, even, than Orestes' matricide,—and one easily atoned for. As Apollo answers the Erinyes in the passage of the *Eumenides* just quoted, 'Bonds can be loosed, therefore there is remedy, and many a means of freedom' (*Eum*, 645). Zeus undid the bonds, made terms with Cronus, and so freed himself from all taint of guilt. In this matter, too, Prometheus seems, at the first hasty view, to have the right on his side, but in the end be is obliged to admit his error.

It has been thought that the central idea of our drama was that of a change in Zeus himself. According to Dissen and Caesar this was the development and purification of Zeus's own character. Keck conceived it as the cessation of a conflict between Zeus and Fate (*Moera*), and the perfecting of Zeus by a union with *Moera*, the personification of eternal law. Welcker's view was that Zeus's nature was changed, in that by making a compact with the son of Themis, or Law, he united Law with himself; and so, from an irresponsible ruler who had attained to power through brute force, be became a wise, just governor, versed in the decrees of eternal Fate, conforming his rule to moral order, and liable no longer to be overthrown. But this transformation of Zeus is an illusion. His milder sway and his more peaceable attitude are not the result of anything in the drama itself, but have their causes quite outside. There is no conflict between Zeus and Fate, only a conflict between a higher and a lower duty. The seeming guilt of Zeus is only a device of the poet, and serves in the end to convince Prometheus and the rest of the world that Zeus from the outset has been a wise and just, though a severe and high-handed ruler. The pious Aeschylus could not possibly have conceived of his supreme god as an originally imperfect being, transformed into a just and wise governor by some outside influence. Some of the gods, no doubt, were thought of as more perfect than others, but that the highest god could undergo discipline and training would have been inconceivable.

The whole plot of the drama turns on the character of Prometheus. By his example it is shown that every revolt against Zeus must necessarily come from ignorance of his wise designs, that every fault imputed to him has its foundation in a purblind and malicious judgment, and that any seeming ground for insubordination, however specious and seductive, must in the end prove a snare and a delusion. This idea the poet has worked out in two connected plays. The *Prometheus Unbound* followed immediately the *Prometheus Bound* in the order of the trilogy.

Personages, Place, and Scenery

The figures of Cratos and Bia were taken by Aeschylus from Hesiod's *Theogony* 385 ff. In the play Bia is only a dumb personage. Her presence would be unnecessary, if Prometheus were not represented by a wooden figure. This figure had to be brought upon the scene; and that this might be done in a manner suitable to the dignity of a god, the poet introduced two brawny forms for the purpose.

Two actors divided the parts between them. The first actor took the parts of Hephaestus and Prometheus; the second, those of Cratos, Oceanus, Io, and Hermes. For Aeschylus at this time still worked under the limitation which was afterwards removed through the influence of Sophocles: only two actors were assigned by the state to each poet for the performance of his plays, and consequently only two speaking personages could be brought upon the stage at any one time. But the poet adapts himself to this restriction very skillfully. At the opening of the play Prometheus is silent until after the exit of Hephaestus. This silence is made necessary by the limitation to two actors; at the same time it is highly characteristic and effective that Prometheus under extreme torture lets no sound of anguish escape him. At 81 Hephaestus retires, while Cratos remains to administer a parting rebuke. This allowed time for the actor of Hephaestus's part, for whom of course no change of dress was necessary, to take his position behind the figure of Prometheus, at the back of the wooden structure built up in front of the rear wall of the stage, to support the movable scenery. Between the several scenes in which Cratos, Oceanus, Io, and Hermes appear, passages of some length are interposed, so that the second actor had time for rest and the assumption of his different costumes.

A not unapt remark about the personages of Aeschylus's plays is found in the citation contained in the Medicean manuscript. 'Aeschylus,' it is there said, 'has this claim to distinction in tragedy, that he introduces great and august persons. In some of his tragedies, indeed, the action is carried on entirely by gods, as in the plays called *Prometheus*: for these dramas are manned by the chiefest of the gods, and the characters upon the stage and the chorus in the orchestra are all divine personages.' Of course these divine personages are represented as acting in all respects according to the laws of human nature.

Upon the place where the scene of the play is laid, the scholiast has rightly concluded that if Io, after leaving Prometheus, is to make a long and devious journey and then arrive at the Caucasus, she cannot be understood as starting from the Caucasus, consequently the Caucasus cannot be the scene of our play. Now the tragedians, at the outset of a play, usually give some indication of the place, so as to assist the imagination of the spectators. But in the *Prometheus [Bound]* no mention is made of the Caucasus; only a dreary, unpeopled region is described, lying at the outermost limit of Scythia (see 117), and near the sea (573), so that Prometheus from his cliff looks out upon the sparkling expanse of water (90, 1088).

Scythia in Aeschylus's time was a generic term for the northern part of the earth, from the Pontus to the Ocean. At the sound of the hammer, as Prometheus is nailed to the rock, the daughters of Oceanus approach: consequently this sea is the Ocean.

The scene of the play is therefore a wild, rocky, desolate region at the ends of the earth, in the north of Scythia close to the Ocean. As the poet departed from the tradition in dividing the time of Prometheus's punishment into two great periods, in order to get, as it were, the frames for two pictures,—so too he has assumed two different places for the punishment, to secure the desirable change of scenery for the second play. The punishment on the Caucasus [in *Prometheus Unbound*] is dramatically heightened by the appearance of the eagle; the earlier punishment [in *Prometheus Bound*] is rendered more impressive by the loneliness of the spot and its remoteness from the civilized world.

The scenery [in *Prometheus Bound*] represents a rocky eminence with a cleft or gorge. The right *periactos* shows the sea, the left a barren mountainous region, intersected perhaps by torrents (89). The figure of Prometheus, after being nailed to the cliff in an upright posture, remains hanging there, rigid and motionless. The wild scenery, the costumes and masks of Cratos and Bia, the smith's tools and the iron clamps and bands with which Hephaestus appears, the ring of the hammer, the extraordinary way in which several of the characters make their entrance,—the Oceanids in a winged chariot, Oceanus riding on a winged steed, and the horned Io suddenly rushing up the rocky slope,—all these worked together to heighten the weird effect of the play and to excite in the spectators mingled feelings of terror, suspense, and compassion.

Editor's Note

Wecklein's introduction is an excellent discussion of the history of the Prometheus myth, of the staging of the plays, and of the issues we must consider to understand this trilogy, but his interpretation of the plays seems to suffer from his conflating Aeschylus' piety with his own piety as a Christian. He describes Zeus in a way that is reminiscent of the Christian idea of divine providence: "Zeus, the powerful far-seeing ruler, who punishes sin relentlessly and imparts 'wisdom through woe' ..., whose eye is bent on the whole and not on details." But Zeus is not so far-seeing as all that: unless Prometheus tells him, he cannot foresee that Thetis will bear a son who will be greater than his father.

Wecklein's main argument for his interpretation is that Zeus must be perfect and unchanging, as he says: "The pious Aeschylus could not possibly have conceived of his supreme god as an originally imperfect being, transformed into a just and wise governor by some outside influence." But the Greeks did not believe their gods were eternal and unchanging, like the Judeo-Christian God, as we can see in the story of the birth of Zeus.

Kronos learned that his sons were fated to overthrow him, just as he had overthrown his father, Uranos. He killed his first five children by swallowing them, but Rhea secretly gave birth to his sixth child, Zeus, in Crete and gave Kronos a stone wrapped in swaddling clothes to swallow. Zeus was hidden in a cave in Crete, while the Kouretes danced, clapped, and shouted, so Kronos could not hear the baby crying.

If Zeus changed from a crying baby to a man who established himself as king by killing his father, isn't it possible that he could have changed further after his kingdom was secure, ultimately becoming the wise ruler whom Aeschylus revered?

We may never be able to fully grasp what pious Greeks thought of their gods, but we can easily see that it is different from what Christians think about God. The story of Io is a prime example: Zeus cheats on his wife, who punishes his lover. No one could possibly conceive of a similar story about the Judeo-Christian God.

Wecklein does give us a summary of other interpretations that are based on the idea that Zeus did change. Though he rejects them, these interpretations have some value.

Nevertheless, Wecklein's view of Zeus is a useful corrective to the impression that we get by reading only *Prometheus Bound* without *Prometheus Unbound*: that Zeus is an arbitrary tyrant, and that Prometheus resists tyranny and will force Zeus to free him as a condition of revealing the prophesy about Thetis. *Prometheus Unbound* begins with the entrance of the chorus of Titans; the fact that Zeus has freed the other Titans shows that he is already more merciful than he was in *Prometheus Bound*, though Prometheus has not intimidated him with this prophesy.

The chapters about *Prometheus Unbound* and *Prometheus the Fire Bearer* contain this edition's interpretation of the trilogy.

—CS

Prometheus Bound
Translated by Henry D. Thoreau[14]

PERSONS OF THE DRAMA
KRATOS and BIA, (Strength and Force)
HEPHAISTUS, (Vulcan)
PROMETHEUS
CHORUS OF OCEAN NYMPHS
OCEANUS
IO, Daughter of Inachus
HERMES

KRATOS and BIA, HEPHAISTUS, PROMETHEUS

Kratos
We are come to the far-bounding plain of earth,
To the Scythian way, to the unapproached solitude.
Hephaistus, orders must have thy attention,
Which the father has enjoined on thee, this bold one
To the high-hanging rocks to bind,
In indissoluble fetters of adamantine bonds.
For thy flower, the splendor of fire useful in all arts,

---

14   First published in the *Dial* magazine, January, 1843. It begins on page 363 of volume 3 of the *Dial*.

Stealing, he bestowed on mortals; and for such
A crime 't is fit he should give satisfaction to the gods;
That he may learn the tyranny of Zeus
To love, and cease from his man-loving ways.

Hephaistus
Kratos and Bia, your charge from Zeus
Already has its end, and nothing further in the way;
But I cannot endure to bind
A kindred god by force to a bleak precipice, —
Yet absolutely there's necessity that I have courage for
                these things;
For it is hard the father's words to banish.
High-plotting son of the right-counseling Themis,
Unwilling thee unwilling in brazen fetters hard to be loosed
I am about to nail to this inhuman hill,
Where neither voice you hear, nor form of any mortal
See, but scorched by the sun's clear flame,
Will change your color's bloom; and to you glad
The various-robed night will conceal the light,
And sun disperse the morning frost again;
And always the burden of the present ill
Will wear you; for he that will relieve you has not yet been
                born.
Such fruits you've reaped from your man-loving ways,
For a god, not shrinking from the wrath of gods,
You have bestowed honors on mortals more than just,
For which this pleasureless rock you'll sentinel,
Standing erect, sleepless, not bending a knee;
And many sighs and lamentations to no purpose
Will you utter; for the mind of Zeus is hard to be changed;
And he is wholly rugged who may newly rule.

Kratos
Well, why cost thou delay and pity in vain?
Why not hate the god most hostile to gods,
Who has betrayed thy prize to mortals?

Hephaistus
The affinity indeed is appalling and the familiarity.

Kratos
I agree, but to disobey the Father's words
How is it possible? Fear you not this more?

Hephaistus
Aye you are always without pity, and full of confidence.

Kratos
For 't is no remedy to bewail this one;
Cherish not vainly troubles which avail nought.

Hephaistus
O much hated handicraft!

Kratos
Why hatest it? for in simple truth, for these misfortunes
Which are present now Art's not to blame.

Hephaistus
Yet I would't had fallen to another's lot.

Kratos
All things were done but to rule the gods,
For none is free but Zeus.

Hephaistus
I knew it, and have nought to say against these things.

Kratos
Will you not haste then to put the bonds about him,
That the Father may not observe you loitering?

Hephaistus
Already at hand the shackles you may see.

Kratos
Taking them, about his hands with firm strength
Strike with the hammer, and nail him to the rocks.

Hephaistus
'T is done, and not in vain this work.

Kratos
Strike harder, tighten, no where relax,
For he is skilful to find out ways e'en from the impracticable.

Hephaistus
Aye but this arm is fixed inextricably.

Kratos
And this now clasp securely; that
He may learn he is a duller schemer than is Zeus.

Hephaistus
Except him would none justly blame me.

Kratos
Now with an adamantine wedge's stubborn fang
Through the breasts nail strongly.

Hephaistus
Alas! alas! Prometheus, I groan for thy afflictions.

Kratos
And do you hesitate, for Zeus' enemies
Do you groan? Beware lest one day you yourself will pity.

Hephaistus
You see a spectacle hard for eyes to behold.

Kratos
I see him meeting his deserts;
But round his sides put straps.

Hephaistus
To do this is necessity, insist not much.

Kratos
Surely I will insist and urge beside,
Go downward, and the thighs surround with force.

Hephaistus
Already it is done, the work, with no long labor.

Kratos
Strongly now drive the fetters, through and through,
For the critic of the works is difficult.

Hephaistus
Like your form your tongue speaks.

Kratos
Be thou softened, but for my stubbornness
Of temper and harshness reproach me not.

Hephaistus
Let us withdraw, for he has a net about his limbs.

Kratos
There now insult, and the shares of gods
Plundering on ephemerals bestow; what thee
Can mortals in these ills relieve?
Falsely thee the divinities Prometheus foreseeing
In what manner you will escape this fortune.

PROMETHEUS, alone.

O divine ether, and ye swift-winged winds,
Fountains of rivers, and countless smilings
Of the ocean waves, and earth, mother of all,
And thou all-seeing orb of the sun I call.
Behold me what a god I suffer at the hands of gods.
See by what outrages
Tormented the myriad-yeared
Time I shall endure; such the new
Ruler of the blessed has contrived for me,
Unseemly bonds.
Alas! alas! the present and the coming
Woe I groan; where ever of these sufferings
Must an end appear.
But what say I? I know beforehand all,
Exactly what will be, nor to me strange
Will any evil come. The destined fate
As easily as possible it behoves to bear, knowing
Necessity's is a resistless strength.
But neither to be silent, nor unsilent about this
Lot is possible for me; for a gift to mortals
Giving, I wretched have been yoked to these necessities;
Within a hollow reed by stealth I carry off fire's

Stolen source, which seemed the teacher
Of all art to mortals, and a great resource.
For such crimes penalty I pay,
Under the sky, riveted in chains.
Ah! ah! alas! alas!
What echo, what odor has flown to me obscure,
Of god, or mortal, or else mingled, —
Came it to this terminal hill
A witness of my sufferings, or wishing what?
Behold bound me an unhappy god,
The enemy of Zeus, fallen under
The ill will of all the gods, as many as
Enter into the hall of Zeus,
Through too great love of mortals.
Alas! alas! what fluttering do I hear
Of birds near? for the air rustles
With the soft rippling of wings.
Everything to me is fearful which creeps this way.

PROMETHEUS and CHORUS.

Chorus
Fear nothing; for friendly this band
Of wings with swift contention
Drew to this hill, hardly
Persuading the paternal mind.
The swift-carrying breezes sent me;
For the echo of beaten steel pierced the recesses
Of the caves, and struck out from me reserved modesty;
And I rushed unsandaled in a winged chariot.

Prometheus
Alas! alas! alas! alas!
Offspring of the fruitful Tethys,

And of him rolling around all
The earth with sleepless stream children,
Of father Ocean; behold, look on me,
By what bonds embraced,
On this cliff's topmost rocks
I shall maintain unenvied watch.

Chorus
I see, Prometheus; but to my eyes a fearful
Mist has come surcharged
With tears, looking upon thy body
Shrunk to the rocks
By these mischiefs of adamantine bonds;
Indeed new helmsmen rule Olympus;
And with new laws Zeus strengthens himself, annulling
      the old,
And the before great now makes unknown.

Prometheus
Would that under earth, and below Hades
Receptacle of dead, to impassible
Tartarus, he had sent me, to bonds indissoluble
Cruelly conducting, that neither god,
Nor any other had rejoiced at this.
But now the sport of winds, unhappy one,
A source of pleasure to my foes I suffer.

Chorus
Who so hard-hearted
Of the gods, to whom these things are pleasant?
Who does not sympathize with thy
Misfortunes, excepting Zeus? for he in wrath always
Fixing his stubborn mind,
Afflicts the heavenly race;
Nor will he cease, until his heart is sated;

Or with some palm some one may take the power hard to
>	be taken.

Prometheus
Surely yet, though in strong
Fetters I am now maltreated,
The ruler of the blessed will have need of me,
To show the new conspiracy, by which
He's robbed of sceptre and of honors,
And not at all me with persuasion's honey-tongued
Charms will he appease, nor ever
Shrinking from his firm threats, will I
Declare this, till from cruel
Bonds he may release, and to do justice
For this outrage be willing.

Chorus
You are bold; and to bitter
Woes do nothing yield,
But too freely speak.
But my mind piercing fear disturbs;
For I'm concerned about thy fortunes,
Where at length arriving you may see
An end of these afflictions. For manners
Inaccessible, and a heart hard to be dissuaded has the son
>	of Kronos.

Prometheus
I know, that Zeus is stern and having
Justice to himself. But after all
Gentle-minded
He will one day be, when thus he's crushed,
And his stubborn wrath allaying,
Into agreement with me and friendliness
Earnest to me earnest he at length will come.

Chorus
The whole account disclose and tell us plainly,
In what crime taking you Zeus
Thus disgracefully and bitterly insults;
Inform us, if you are nowise hurt by the recital.

Prometheus
Painful indeed it is to me to tell these things,
And a pain to be silent, and every way unfortunate.
When first the divinities began their strife,
And discord 'mong themselves arose,
Some wishing to cast out Kronos from his seat,
That Zeus might reign, forsooth, others the contrary
Striving, that Zeus might never rule the gods;
Then I the best advising, to persuade
The Titans, sons of Uranus and Chthon,
Unable was; but crafty stratagems
Despising with rude minds,
They thought without trouble to rule by force;
But to me my mother not once only, Themis,
And Gaia, of many names one form,
How the future should be accomplished had foretold,
That not by power, nor by strength
Would it be necessary, but by craft the victors should
     prevail.
Such I in words expounding,
They deigned not to regard at all.
The best course therefore of those occurring then
Appeared to be, taking my mother to me,
Of my own accord to side with Zeus glad to receive me;
And by my counsels Tartarus' black-pitted
Depth conceals the ancient Kronos,
With his allies. In such things by me
The tyrant of the gods having been helped,

With base rewards like these repays me,
For there is somehow in kingship
This disease, not to trust its friends.
What then you ask, for what cause
He afflicts me, this will I now explain.
As soon as on his father's throne
He sat, he straightway to the gods distributes honors,
Some to one and to another some, and arranged
The government; but of unhappy mortals account
Had none; but blotting out the race
Entire, wished to create another new.
And these things none opposed but I,
But I adventured; I rescued mortals
From going destroyed to Hades.
Therefore indeed with such afflictions am I bent,
To suffer grievous, and piteous to behold,
And holding mortals up to pity, myself am not
Thought worthy to obtain it; but without pity
Am I thus corrected, a spectacle inglorious to Zeus,
Of iron heart and made of stone.

Chorus
Whoe'er, Prometheus, with thy sufferings
Does not grieve; for I should not have wished to see
These things, and having seen them I grieved at heart.

Prometheus
Indeed to friends I'm piteous to behold.

Chorus
Did you in no respect go beyond this?

Prometheus
True, mortals I made cease foreseeing fate.

Chorus
Having found what remedy for this ail?

Prometheus
Blind hopes in them I made to dwell.

Chorus
A great advantage this you gave to men

Prometheus
Beside these, too, I bestowed on them fire.

Chorus
And have mortals flamy fire?

Prometheus
From which indeed they will learn many arts.

Chorus
Upon such charges then does Zeus
Maltreat you, and nowhere relax from ills?
Is there no term of suffering lying before thee?

Prometheus
Nay, none at all, but when to him it may seem good.

Chorus
And how will it seem good? What hope?
See you not that
You have erred? But how you've erred, for me to tell
Not pleasant, and to you a pain. But these things
Let us omit, and seek you some release from sufferings.

Prometheus
Easy, whoever out of trouble holds his

Foot, to admonish and remind those faring
Ill. But all these things I knew,
Willing, willing I erred, I'll not deny;
Mortals assisting I myself found trouble.
Not indeed with penalties like these thought I
That I should pine on lofty rocks,
Gaining this drear unneighbored hill.
But bewail not my present woes,
But alighting, the fortunes creeping on
Hear ye, that ye may learn all to the end.
Obey me, obey, sympathize
With him now suffering. Thus indeed affliction
Wandering round, sits now by one, then by another.

Chorus
Not to unwilling ears do you urge
This, Prometheus.
And now with light foot the swift- rushing
Seat leaving, and the pure ether,
Path of birds, to this peaked
Ground I come; for thy misfortunes
I wish fully to hear.

PROMETHEUS, CHORUS, and OCEANUS.

Oceanus
I come to the end of a long way
Travelling to thee, Prometheus,
By my will without bits directing
This wing-swift bird;
For at thy fortunes know I grieve.
And, I think, affinity thus
Impels me, but apart from birth,

There's not to whom a higher rank
I would assign than thee.
And you will know these things as true and not in vain
To flatter with the tongue is in me.
Come, therefore,
Show how it is necessary to assist you;
For never will you say, than Ocean
There's a firmer friend to thee.

Prometheus
Alas! what now? And you then of my sufferings
Come spectator? How didst thou dare, leaving
The stream which bears thy name, and rock-roofed
Caves self-built, to the iron-mother
Earth to go? To behold my fate
Hast come, and to compassionate my ills?
Behold a spectacle, this, the friend of Zeus,
Having with him stablished his tyranny,
With what afflictions by himself I'm bent.

Oceanus
I see, Prometheus, and would admonish
Thee the best, although of varied craft.
Know thyself, and fit thy manners
New; for new also the king among the gods.
But if thus rude and whetted words
Thou wilt hurl out, quickly may Zeus, though sitting
Far above, hear thee, so that thy present wrath
Of troubles child's play will seem to be.
But, O wretched one, dismiss the indignation which thou
                hast,
And seek deliverance from these woes.
Like an old man, perhaps, I seem to thee to say these things;
Such, however, are the wages
Of the too lofty speaking tongue, Prometheus,

But thou art not yet humble, nor dost yield to ills,
And beside the present wish to receive others still.
But thou wouldst not, with my counsel,
Against the pricks extend your limbs, seeing that
A stern monarch, irresponsible reigns.
And now I go, and will endeavor,
If I can, to release thee from these sufferings.
But be thou quiet, nor too rudely speak.
Know'st thou not well, with thy superior wisdom, that
On a vain tongue punishment is inflicted?

Prometheus
I congratulate thee that thou art without blame,
Having shared and dared all with me,
And now leave off, and let it not concern thee.
For altogether thou wilt not persuade him, for he's not
           easily persuaded,
But take heed yourself lest you be injured by the way.

Oceanus
Far better thou art to advise those near
Than thyself; by deed and not by word I judge.
But me hastening by no means mayest thou detain,
For I boast, I boast, this favor will Zeus
Grant me, from these sufferings to release thee.
So far I praise thee, and will never cease;
For zeal you nothing lack. But
Strive not; for in vain, nought helping
Me, thou'lt strive, if aught to strive you wish.
But be thou quiet, holding thyself aloof,
For I would not, though I'm unfortunate, that on this account
Evils should come to many.

Prometheus
Surely not, for me too the fortunes of thy brother
Atlas grieve, who towards the evening-places
Stands, the pillar of heaven and earth
Upon his shoulders bearing, a load not easy to be borne.
And the earth-born inhabitant of the Cilician
Caves, seeing, I pitied, the savage monster
With a hundred heads, by force o'ercome,
Typhon impetuous, who stood 'gainst all the gods,
With frightful jaws hissing out slaughter;
And from his eyes flashed a gorgonian light,
Utterly to destroy by force the sovereignty of Zeus;
But there came to him Zeus' sleepless bolt,
Descending thunder, breathing flame,
Which struck him out from lofty
Boastings. For struck to his very heart,
His strength was scorched and thundered out.
And now a useless and extended carcass
Lies he near a narrow passage of the sea,
Pressed down under the roots of Etna.
And on the topmost summit seated, Hephaistus
Hammers the ignited mass, whence will burst out at length
Rivers of fire, devouring with wild jaws
Fair-fruited Sicily's smooth fields;
Such rage will Typhon make boil over
With hot discharges of insatiable fire-breathing tempest,
Though by the bolt of Zeus burnt to a coal.
Thou art not inexperienced, nor dost want
My counsel; secure thyself as thou know'st how;
And I against the present fortune will bear up,
Until the thought of Zeus may cease from wrath.

Oceanus
Know'st thou not this, Prometheus, that

Words are healers of distempered wrath?

Prometheus
If any seasonably soothe the heart,
And swelling passion check not rudely.

Oceanus
In the consulting and the daring
What harm seest thou existing? Teach me.

Prometheus
Trouble superfluous, and light-minded folly.

Oceanus
Be this my ail then, since it is
Most profitable being wise not to seem wise.

Prometheus
This will seem to be my error.

Oceanus
Plainly homeward thy words remand me.

Prometheus
Aye, let not grief for me into hostility cast thee.

Oceanus
To the new occupant of the all-powerful seats?

Prometheus
Beware lest ever his heart be angered.

Oceanus
Thy fate, Prometheus, is my teacher.

Prometheus
Go thou, depart, preserve the present mind.

Oceanus
To me rushing this word you utter.
For the smooth path of the air sweeps with his wings
The four-legged bird; and gladly would
In the stalls at home bend a knee.

PROMETHEUS and CHORUS.

Chorus
I mourn for thee thy ruinous
Fate, Prometheus,
And tear-distilling from my tender
Eyes a stream has wet
My cheeks with flowing springs;
For these, unenvied, Zeus
By his own laws enforcing,
Haughty above the gods
That were displays his sceptre.
And every region now
With groans resounds,
Mourning the illustrious
And ancient honor
Of thee and of thy kindred;
As many mortals as the habitable seat
Of sacred Asia pasture,
With thy lamentable
Woes have sympathy.
And of the Colchian land, virgin
Inhabitants, in fight undaunted,
And Scythia's multitude, who the last

Place of earth, about
Maeotis lake possess,
And Arabia's martial flower,
And who the high-hung citadels
Of Caucasus inhabit near,
A hostile army, raging
With sharp-pronged spears.
Only one other god before, in sufferings
Subdued by injuries
Of adamantine bonds, I've seen, Titanian
Atlas, who always with superior strength
The huge and heavenly globe
On his back bears;
And with a roar the sea waves
Dashing, groans the deep,
And the dark depth of Hades murmurs underneath
The earth, and fountains of pure-running rivers
Heave a pitying sigh.

Prometheus
Think not indeed through weakness or through pride
That I am silent; for with the consciousness I gnaw my heart,
Seeing myself thus basely used.
And yet to these new gods their shares
Who else than I wholly distributed?
But of these things I am silent; for I should tell you
What you know; the sufferings of mortals too
You've heard, how I made intelligent
And possessed of sense them ignorant before.
But I will speak, not bearing any grudge to men,
But showing in what I gave the good intention;
At first, indeed, seeing they saw in vain,
And hearing heard not; but like the forms
Of dreams, for that long time, rashly confounded

All, nor brick-woven dwellings
Knew they, placed in the sun, nor wood-work;
But digging down they dwelt, like puny
Ants, in sunless nooks of caves.
And there was nought to them, neither of winter sign,
Nor of flower-giving spring, nor fruitful
Summer, that was sure; but without knowledge
Did they all, till I taught them the risings
Of the stars, and goings down, hard to determine.
And numbers, chief of inventions,
I found out for them, and the assemblages of letters,
And memory, Muse-mother, doer of all things,
And first I joined in pairs wild animals
Obedient to the yoke; and that they might be
Alternate workers with the bodies of men
In the severest toils, harnessed the rein-loving horses
To the car, the ornament of over-wealthy luxury.
And none else than I invented the sea-wandering
Flaxen-winged vehicles of sailors.
Such inventions I wretched having found out
For men, myself have not the ingenuity by which
From the now present ill I may escape.

Chorus
You suffer unseemly ill, deranged in mind
You err; and as some bad physician, falling
Sick you are dejected, and cannot find
By what remedies you may be healed.

Prometheus
Hearing the rest from me more will you wonder,
What arts and what expedients I planned.
That which was greatest, if any might fall sick,
There was alleviation none, neither to eat,
Nor to anoint, nor drink, but for the want

Of medicines they were reduced to skeletons, till to them
I showed the mingling of mild remedies,
By which all ails they drive away.
And many modes of prophecy I settled,
And distinguished first of dreams what a real
Vision is required to be, and omens hard to be determined
I made known to them; and tokens by the way,
And flight of crooked-taloned birds I accurately
Defined, which lucky are,
And unlucky, and what mode of life
Have each, and to one another what
Hostilities, attachments, and assemblings;
The entrails' smoothness, and what color having
They would be to the divinities acceptable,
Of the gall and liver the various symmetry,
And the limbs concealed in fat; and the long
Flank burning, to an art hard to be guessed
I showed the way to mortals; and flammeous signs
Explained, before obscure.
Such indeed these; and under ground
Concealed the helps to men,
Brass, iron, silver, gold, who
Would affirm that he discovered before me?
None, I well know, not wishing in vain to boast.
But learn all in one word,
All arts to mortals from Prometheus.

Chorus
Assist not mortals now unseasonably,
And neglect yourself unfortunate; for I
Am of good hope, that from these bonds
Released, you will yet have no less
power than Zeus.

Prometheus
Never thus has Fate the Accomplisher
Decreed to fulfill these things, but by a myriad ills
And woes subdued, thus bonds I flee;
For art's far weaker than necessity.

Chorus
Who then is helmsman of necessity?

Prometheus
The Fates three-formed, and the remembering Furies.

Chorus
Than these then is Zeus weaker?

Prometheus
Aye, he could not escape what has been fated.

Chorus
But what to Zeus is fated, except always to rule?

Prometheus
This thou wilt not learn; seek not to know.

Chorus
Surely some awful thing it is which you withhold.

Prometheus
Remember other words, for this by no means
Is it time to tell, but to be concealed
As much as possible; for keeping this do I
Escape unseemly bonds and woes.

Chorus
Never may the all-ruling
Zeus put into my mind
Force antagonist to him.
Nor let me cease drawing near
The gods with holy sacrifices
Of slain oxen, by Father Ocean's
Ceaseless passage,
Nor offend with words,
But in me this remain,
And ne'er be melted out.
'T is something sweet with bold
Hopes the long life to
Extend, in bright
Cheerfulness cherishing the spirit.
But I shudder, thee beholding
By a myriad sufferings
tormented.
For not fearing Zeus,
In thy private mind thou dost regard
Mortals too much, Prometheus.
Come, though a thankless
Favor, friend, say where is any strength,
From ephemerals any help? Saw you not
The powerless inefficiency,
Dream-like, in which the blind
Race of mortals are entangled?
Never counsels of mortals
May transgress the harmony of Zeus.
I learned these things looking on
Thy destructive fate, Prometheus.
For different to me did this strain come,
And that which round thy baths
And couch I hymned,

With the design of marriage, when my father's child
With bridal gifts persuading, thou didst lead
Hesione the partner of thy bed.

PROMETHEUS, CHORUS, and IO.

Io
What earth, what race, what being shall I say is this
I see in bridles of rock
Exposed? By what crime's
Penalty dost thou perish? Show, to what part
Of earth I miserable have wandered.
Ah! ah! alas! alas!
Again some fly doth sting me wretched,
Image of earth-born Argus, cover it earth;
I fear the myriad-eyed herdsman beholding;
For he goes having a treacherous eye,
Whom not e'en dead the earth conceals.
But me, wretched from the Infernals passing,
He pursues, and drives fasting along the sea-side
Sand, while low resounds a wax-compacted reed,
Uttering sleep-giving law; alas! alas! O gods!
Where, gods! where lead me far-wandering courses?
In what sin, O son of Kronos, In what sin ever having taken,
To these afflictions hast thou yoked me? alas! alas!
With fly-driven fear a wretched
Phrenzied one dost thus afflict?
With fire burn, or with earth cover, or
To sea monsters give for food, nor
Envy me my prayers, king.
Enough much-wandered wanderings
Have exercised me, nor can I learn where
I shall escape from sufferings.

Chorus
Hear'st thou the address of the cow-horned virgin?

Prometheus
And how not hear the fly-whirled virgin,
Daughter of Inachus, who Zeus' heart warmed
With love, and now the courses over long,
By Here hated, forcedly performs?

Io
Whence utterest thou my father's name,
Tell me, miserable, who thou art,
That to me, O suffering one, me born to suffer,
Thus true things dost address?
The god-sent ail thou'st named,
Which wastes me stinging
With maddening goads, alas! alas!
With foodless and unseemly leaps
Rushing headlong, I came,
By wrathful plots subdued.
Who of the wretched, who, alas! alas! suffers like me?
But to me clearly show
What me awaits to suffer,
What not necessary; what remedy of ill,
Teach, if indeed thou know'st, speak out,
Tell the ill-wandering virgin.

Prometheus
I'll clearly tell thee all you wish to learn.
Not weaving in enigmas, but in simple speech,
As it is just to open the mouth to friends.
Thou seest the giver of fire to men, Prometheus.

Io
O thou who didst appear a common help to mortals,

Wretched Prometheus, to atone for what do you endure
this?

Prometheus
I have scarce ceased my sufferings lamenting.

Io
Would you not grant this favor to me?

Prometheus
Say what you ask; for you'd learn all from me.

Io
Say who has bound thee to the cliff.

Prometheus
The will indeed of Zeus, Hephaistus' the hand.

Io
And penalty for what crimes dost thou pay?

Prometheus
Thus much only can I show thee.

Io
But beside this, declare what time will be
To me unfortunate the limit of my wandering.

Prometheus
Not to learn is better for thee than to learn these things.

Io
Conceal not from me what I am to suffer.

Prometheus
Indeed, I grudge thee not this favor.

Io
Why then dost thou delay to tell the whole?

Prometheus
There's no unwillingness, but I hesitate to vex thy mind.

Io
Care not for me more than is pleasant to me.

Prometheus
Since you are earnest, it behoves to speak; hear then.

Chorus
Not yet indeed; but a share of pleasure also give to me.
First we'll learn the malady of this one,
Herself relating her destructive fortunes,
And the remainder of her trials let her learn from thee.

Prometheus
'T is thy part, Io, to do these a favor,
As well for every other reason, and as they are sisters of
                          thy father.
Since to weep and to lament misfortunes,
There where one will get a tear
From those attending, is worth the delay.

Io
I know not that I need distrust you,
But in plain speech you shall learn
All that you ask for; and yet e'en telling I lament
The god-sent tempest, and dissolution
Of my form, whence to me miserable it came.

For always visions in the night moving about
My virgin chambers, enticed me
With smooth words; "O greatly happy virgin,
Why be a virgin long? it is permitted to obtain
The greatest marriage. For Zeus with love's dart
Has been warmed by thee, and wishes to unite
In love; but do thou, O child, spurn not the couch
Of Zeus, but go out to Lerna's deep
Morass, and stables of thy father's herds,
That the divine eye may cease from desire."
With such dreams every night
Was I unfortunate distressed, till I dared tell
My father of the night-wandering visions.
And he to Pytho and Dodona frequent
Prophets sent, that he might learn what it was necessary
He should say or do, to do agreeably to the gods.
And they came bringing ambiguous
Oracles, darkly and indistinctly uttered.
But finally a plain report came to Inachus,
Clearly enjoining him and telling,
Out of my home and country to expel me,
Discharged to wander to the earth's last bounds,
And if he was not willing, from Zeus would come
A fiery thunderbolt, which would annihilate all his race.
Induced by such predictions of the Loxian,
Against his will he drove me out unwilling,
And shut me from the houses; but Zeus' rein
Compelled him by force to do these things.
Immediately my form and mind were
Changed, and horned, as you behold, stung
By a sharp-mouthed fly, with frantic leaping
Rushed I to Cenchrea's palatable stream,
And Lerna's source; but a herdsman born-of-earth
Of violent temper, Argus, accompanied, with numerous

Eyes my steps observing.
But unexpectedly a sudden fate
Robbed him of life; and I, fly-stung,
By lash divine am driven from land to land.
You hear what has been done; and if you have to say,
What's left of labors, speak; nor pitying me
Comfort with false words; for an ill
The worst of all, I say, are made-up words.

Chorus
Ah! ah! enough, alas!
Ne'er, ne'er did I presume such cruel words
Would reach my ears, nor thus unsightly,
And intolerable hurts, sufferings, fears with a two-edged
Goad would chill my soul;
Alas! alas! fate! fate!
I shudder, seeing the state of Io.

Prometheus
Before hand sigh'st thou, and art full of fears,
Hold till the rest also thou learn'st.

Chorus
Tell, teach; for to the sick 't is sweet
To know the remaining pain beforehand clearly.

Prometheus
Your former wish ye got from me
With ease; for first ye asked to learn from her
Relating her own trials;
The rest now hear, what sufferings 't is necessary
This young woman should endure from Here.
But do thou, offspring of Inachus, my words
Cast in thy mind, that thou may'st learn the boundaries of
            the way.

First, indeed, hence toward the rising of the sun
Turning thyself, travel uncultivated lands,
And to the Scythian nomads thou wilt come, who woven
                                     roofs
On high inhabit, on well-wheeled carts.
With far-casting bows equipped;
Whom go not near, but to the sea-resounding cliffs
Bending thy feet, pass from the region.
On the left hand the iron-working
Chalybes inhabit, whom thou must needs beware,
For they are rude and inaccessible to strangers.
And thou wilt come to the Hybristes river, not ill named,
Which pass not, for not easy is't to pass,
Before you get to Caucasus itself, highest
Of mountains, where the stream spurts out its tide
From the very temples; and passing over
The star-neighbored summits, 't is necessary to go,
The southern way where thou wilt come to the man-hating
Army of the Amazons, who Themiscyra one day
Will inhabit, by the Thermodon, where's
Salmydessia, rough jaw of the sea,
Inhospitable to sailors, step-mother of ships;
They will conduct thee on thy way, and very cheerfully.
And to the Cimmerian isthmus thou wilt come,
Just on the narrow portals of a lake, which leaving
It behoves thee with stout heart to pass the Maeotic straits;
And there will be to mortals ever a great fame
Of thy passage, and Bosphorus from thy name
'T will be called. And leaving Europe's plain
The continent of Asia thou wilt reach. Seemeth to thee,
                                     forsooth,
The tyrant of the gods in everything to be
Thus violent? For he a god with this mortal
Wishing to unite, drove her to these wanderings.

A bitter wooer didst thou find, O virgin,
For thy marriage. For the words you now have heard
Think not yet to be the prelude.

Io
Ah! me! me! alas! alas!

Prometheus
Again dost shriek and heave a sigh? What
Wilt thou do when the remaining ills thou learn'st?

Chorus
And hast thou any further suffering to tell her?

Prometheus
Aye, a tempestuous sea of baleful woe.

Io
What profit then for me to live, and not in haste
To cast myself from this rough rock,
That rushing down upon the plain I may be released
From every trouble? For better once for all to die,
Than all my days to suffer evilly.

Prometheus
Unhappily my trials would'st thou bear,
To whom to die has not been fated;
For this would be release from sufferings;
But now there is no end of ills lying
Before me, until Zeus falls from sovereignty.

Io
And is Zeus ever to fall from power?

Prometheus
Thou would'st be pleased, I think, to see this accident.

Io
How should I not, who suffer ill from Zeus?

Prometheus
That these things then are so, be thou assured.

Io
By what one will the tyrant's power be robbed?

Prometheus
Himself, by his own senseless counsels.

Io
In what way show, if there's no harm.

Prometheus
He will make such a marriage as one day he'll repent.

Io
Of god or mortal? If to be spoken, tell.

Prometheus
What matter which? For these things are not to be told.

Io
By a wife will he be driven from the throne?

Prometheus
Aye, she will bring forth a son superior to his father.

Io
Is there no refuge for him from this fate?

Prometheus
None, surely, till I may be released from bonds.

Io
Who then is to release thee, Zeus unwilling?

Prometheus
He must be some one of thy descendants.

Io
How sayest thou-that my child will deliver thee from ills?

Prometheus
Third of thy race after ten other births.

Io
This oracle is not yet easy to be guessed.

Prometheus
But do not seek to understand thy sufferings.

Io
First proffering gain to me, do not then withhold it.

Prometheus
I'll grant thee one of two relations.

Io
What two propose, and give to me my choice.

Prometheus
I give; choose whether thy remaining troubles
I shall tell thee clearly, or him that will release me.

Chorus
Consent to do her the one favor,
Me the other, nor deem us undeserving of thy words;
To her indeed tell what remains of wandering,
And to me, who will release; for I desire this.

Prometheus
Since ye are earnest, I will not resist
To tell the whole, as much as ye ask. I
To thee first, Io, vexatious wandering will tell,
Which engrave on the remembering tablets of the mind.
When thou hast passed the flood, boundary of continents,
Towards the flaming orient sun-travelled
Passing through the tumult of the sea until you reach
The gorgonean plains of Cisthene, where
The Phorcides dwell, old virgins,
Three, swan-shaped, having a common eye,
One-toothed, whom neither the sun looks on
With his beams, nor nightly moon eyes
And near, their winged sisters three,
Dragon-scaled Gorgons, odious to men
Whom no mortal beholding, will have breath;
Such danger do I tell thee,
But hear another odious sight;
Beware the gryphons, sharp-mouthed
Dogs of Zeus, which bark not, and the one-eyed Arimaspian
Host, going on horse-back, who dwell about
The golden-flowing flood of Pluto's channel;
These go not near. But to a distant land
Thou'lt come, a dusky race, who near the fountains
Of the sun inhabit, where is the Aethiopian river.
Creep down the banks of this, until thou com'st
To a descent, where from Byblinian mounts
The Nile sends down its sacred palatable stream.

This will conduct thee to the triangled land
Nilean, where, Io, 't is decreed
Thou and thy progeny shall form the distant colony.
If aught of this is unintelligible to thee, and hard to be
                found out,
Repeat thy questions, and learn clearly;
For more leisure than I want is granted me.

Chorus
If to her aught remaining or omitted
Thou hast to tell of her pernicious wandering,
Speak; but if thou hast said all, give us
The favor which we ask, for surely thou remember'st.

Prometheus
The whole term of her travelling has she heard.
But that she may know that not in vain she hears me,
I'll tell what before coming hither she endured,
Giving this as proof of my relations.
The great multitude of words I will omit,
And proceed unto the very limit of thy wanderings.
When then you came to the Molossian ground,
And near the high-ridged Dodona, where
Oracle and seat is of Thesprotian Zeus,
And prodigy incredible, the speaking oaks,
By whom thou clearly, and nought enigmatically,
Wert called the illustrious wife of Zeus
About to be, if aught of these things soothes thee;
Thence, driven by the fly, you came
The seaside way to the great gulf of Rhea,
From which by courses retrograde you are now tempest-
                tossed.
But for time to come the sea gulf,
Clearly know, will be called Ionian,
Memorial of thy passage to all mortals.

Proofs to thee are these of my intelligence,
That it sees somewhat more than the apparent.
But the rest to you and her in common I will tell,
Having come upon the very track of former words.
There is a city Canopus, last of the land,
By Nile's very mouth and bank;
There at length Zeus makes thee sane,
Stroking with gentle hand, and touching only.
And, named from Zeus' begetting,
Thou wilt bear dark Epaphus, who will reap
As much land as broad-flowing Nile doth water;
And fifth from him, a band of fifty children
Again to Argos shall unwilling come,
Of female sex, avoiding kindred marriage
Of their cousins; but they, with minds inflamed,
Hawks by doves not far left behind,
Will come pursuing marriages
Not to be pursued, but heaven will take vengeance on their
 bodies;
For them Pelasgia shall receive by Mars
Subdued with woman's hand with night-watching boldness.
For each wife shall take her husband's life,
Staining a two-edged dagger in his throat.
Such 'gainst my foes may Cypris come.
But one of the daughters shall love soften
Not to slay her bed-fellow, but she will waver
In her mind; and one of two things will prefer,
To hear herself called timid, rather than stained with blood;
She shall in Argos bear a royal race.
Of a long speech is need this clearly to discuss.
From this seed, however, shall be born a brave,
Famed for his bow, who will release me
From these sufferings. Such oracle my ancient
Mother told me, Titanian Themis;

But how and by what means, this needs long speech
To tell, and nothing, learning, wilt thou gain.

Io
Ah me! ah wretched me!
Spasms again and brain-struck
Madness burn me within, and a fly's dart
Stings me not wrought by fire.
My heart with fear knocks at my breast,
And my eyes whirl round and round,
And from my course I'm borne by madness'
Furious breath, unable to control my tongue;
While confused words dash idly
'Gainst the waves of horrid woe.

Chorus
Wise, wise indeed was he,
Who first in mind
This weighed, and with the tongue expressed,
To marry according to one's degree is best by far;
Nor being a laborer with the hands,
To woo those who are by wealth corrupted,
Nor those by birth made great.
Never, never me Fates
May you behold the sharer of Zeus' couch.
Nor may I be brought near to any husband among those
    from heaven,
For I fear, seeing the virginhood of Io,
Not content with man, through marriage vexed
With these distressful wanderings by Here.
But for myself, since an equal marriage is without fear,
I am not concerned lest the love of the almighty
Gods cast its inevitable eye on me.
Without war indeed this war, producing

Troubles; nor do I know what would become of me;
For I see not how I should escape the subtlety of Zeus.

Prometheus
Surely shall Zeus, though haughty now,
Yet be humble, such marriage
He prepares to make, which from sovereignty
And the throne will cast him down obscure; and father Kronos'
Curse will then be all fulfilled,
Which falling from the ancient seats he imprecated.
And refuge from such ills none of the gods
But I can show him clearly.
I know these things, and in what manner. Now therefore
Being bold, let him sit trusting to lofty
Sounds, and brandishing with both hands his fire-breathing weapon,
For nought will these avail him, not
To fall disgracefully intolerable falls;
Such wrestler does he now prepare,
Himself against himself, a prodigy most hard to be withstood;
Who, indeed, will invent a better flame than lightning,
And a loud sound surpassing thunder;
And shiver the trident, Neptune's weapon,
The marine earth-shaking ail.
Stumbling upon this ill he'll learn
How different to govern and to serve.

Chorus
Aye, as you hope you vent this against Zeus.

Prometheus
What will be done, and also what I hope, I say.

Chorus
And are we to expect that any will rule Zeus?

Prometheus
Even than these more grievous ills he'll have.

Chorus
How fear'st thou not, hurling such words?

Prometheus
What should I fear, to whom to die has not been fated?

Chorus
But suffering more grievous still than this he may inflict.

Prometheus
Then let him do it; all is expected by me.

Chorus
Those reverencing Adrastia are wise.

Prometheus
Revere, pray, flatter each successive ruler.
Me less than nothing Zeus concerns.
Let him do, let him prevail this short time
As he will, for long he will not rule the gods.
But I see here, indeed, Zeus' runner,
The new tyrant's drudge;
Doubtless he brings us some new message.

PROMETHEUS, CHORUS, and HERMES.

Hermes
To thee, the sophist, the bitterly bitter,

The sinner against gods, the giver of honors
To ephemerals, the thief of fire
The father commands thee to tell the marriage
Which you boast, by which he falls from power;
And that too not enigmatically,
But each particular declare; nor cause me
Double journeys, Prometheus; for thou see'st that
Zeus is not appeased by such.

Prometheus
Solemn-mouthed and full of wisdom
Is thy speech, as of the servant of the gods.
Ye newly rule, and think forsooth
To dwell in griefless citadels; have I not seen
Two tyrants fallen from these?
And third I shall behold him ruling now,
Basest and speediest. Do I seem to thee
To fear and shrink from the new gods?
Nay, much and wholly I fall short of this.
The way thou cam'st go through the dust again;
For thou wilt learn nought which thou ask'st of me.

Hermes
Aye, by such insolence before
You brought yourself into these woes.

Prometheus
Plainly know, I would not change
My ill fortune for thy servitude,
For better, I think, to serve this rock
Than be the faithful messenger of Father Zeus.
Thus to insult the insulting it is fit.

Hermes
Thou seem'st to enjoy thy present state.

Prometheus
I enjoy? Enjoying thus my enemies
Would I see; and thee 'mong them I count.

Hermes
Dost thou blame me for aught of thy misfortunes?

Prometheus
In plain words, all gods I hate,
As many as well treated wrong me unjustly.

Hermes
I hear thee raving, no slight ail.

Prometheus
Aye, I should ail, if ail one's foes to hate.

Hermes
If prosperous, thou couldst not be borne.

Prometheus
Ah me!

Hermes
This word Zeus does not know.

Prometheus
But time growing old teaches all things.

Hermes
And still thou know'st not yet how to be prudent.

Prometheus
For I should not converse with thee a servant.

Hermes
Thou seem'st to say nought which the father wishes.

Prometheus
And yet his debtor I'd requite the favor.

Hermes
Thou mock'st me verily as if I were a child.

Prometheus
And art thou not a child, and simpler still than this,
If thou expectest to learn aught from me?
There is not outrage nor expedient, by which
Zeus will induce me to declare these things,
Before he loose these grievous bonds.
Let there be hurled then flaming fire,
And with white-winged snows, and thunders
Of the earth, let him confound and mingle all.
For none of these will bend me till I tell
By whom 't is necessary he should fall from sovereignty.

Hermes
Consider now if these things seem helpful.

Prometheus
Long since these were considered and resolved.

Hermes
Venture, O vain one, venture, at length,
In view of present sufferings to be wise.

Prometheus
In vain you vex me, as a wave, exhorting.
Ne'er let it come into thy mind, that, I, fearing
Zeus' anger, shall become woman-minded,
And beg him, greatly hated,
With womanish upturnings of the hands,
To loose me from these bonds. I am far from it.

Hermes
Though saying much I seem in vain to speak;
For thou art nothing softened nor appeased
By prayers; but champing at the bit like a new-yoked
Colt, thou strugglest and contend'st against the reins.
But thou art violent with feeble wisdom
For stubbornness to him who is not wise,
Itself alone, is less than nothing strong.
But consider, if thou art not persuaded by my words,
What storm and triple surge of ills
Will come upon thee not to be avoided for first this rugged
Cliff with thunder and lightning flame
The Father'll rend, and hide
Thy body, and a strong arm will bury thee.
When thou hast spent a long length of time,
Thou wilt come back to light; and Zeus'
Winged dog, a blood-thirsty eagle, ravenously
Shall tear the great rag of thy body,
Creeping an uninvited guest all day,
And banquet on thy liver black by eating.
Of such suffering expect not any end,
Before some god appear
Succeeding to thy labors, and wish to go to rayless
Hades, and the dark depths of Tartarus.
Therefore deliberate; since this is not made
Boasting, but in earnest spoken;

For to speak falsely does not know the mouth
Of Zeus, but every word he does. So
Look about thee, and consider, nor ever think
Obstinacy better than prudence.

Chorus
To us indeed Hermes appears to say not unseasonable
                    things,
For he directs thee, leaving off
Self-will, to seek prudent counsel.
Obey; for, it is base for a wise man to err.

Prometheus
To me foreknowing these messages
He has uttered, but for a foe to suffer ill
From foes, is nought unseemly.
Therefore 'gainst me let there be hurled
Fire's double-pointed curl, and air
Be provoked with thunder, and a tumult
Of wild winds; and earth from its foundations
Let a wind rock, and its very roots,
And with a rough surge mingle
The sea waves with the passages
Of the heavenly stars, and to black
Tartarus let him quite cast down my
Body, by necessity's strong eddies;
Yet after all he will not kill me.

Hermes
Such words and counsels you may hear
From the brain-struck.
For what lacks he of being mad?
And if prosperous, what does he ceas' from madness?
Do you, therefore, who sympathize
With this one's suffering,

From these places quick withdraw somewhere,
Lest the harsh bellowing of thunder
Stupify your minds.

Chorus
Say something else, and exhort me
To some purpose; for surely
Thou hast intolerably abused this word.
How direct me to perform a baseness,
I wish to suffer with him whate'er is necessary,
For I have learned to hate betrayers;
Nor is there pest
Which I abominate more than this.

Hermes
Remember then what I fore-tell;
Nor by calamity pursued
Blame fortune, nor e'er say
That Zeus into unforeseen
Ill has cast you; surely not, but yourselves
You yourselves; for knowing,
And not suddenly nor clandestinely,
You'll be entangled through your folly
In an impassible net of woe.

Prometheus
Surely in deed, and no more in word,
Earth is shaken;
And a hoarse sound of thunder
Bellows near, and wreaths of lightning
Flash out fiercely blazing, and whirlwinds dust
Whirl up; and leap the blasts
Of all winds, 'gainst one another
Blowing in opposite array;

And air with sea is mingled;
Such impulse against me from Zeus
Producing fear, doth plainly come.
O revered Mother, O Ether,
Revolving common light to all,
You see me, how unjust things I endure!

Prometheus Unbound
Description and Fragments

Though relatively few fragments remain from *Prometheus Unbound*, we can reconstruct much of the play's action from these fragments and from foreshadowings in *Prometheus Bound*. This section includes a description of the action of *Prometheus Unbound* with the surviving fragments in the appropriate locations.

The Action and Fragments

The play begins as the chorus of Titans enters. Zeus had imprisoned Kronos and these Titans in Tartarus after Zeus and the Olympian gods defeated the Titans in a war that lasted ten years. Now, he has released the Titans, who come to the place where Prometheus (himself a Titan) is bound to a rock in the Caucasus. The Titans greet Prometheus and describe their journey.

> **Fragment 1:**
> Aeschylus ... in the tragedy of *Prometheus Delivered* ...introduces the Titans speaking thus to Prometheus:
> "Hither are we come to see thy labours, O Prometheus! and the sufferings which thou undergoest in consequence of thy bonds"

and in specifying how large a space of ground they had passed over in their journey, they speak of the Phasis as

"the twin-born offspring of the earth and the great boundary of Europe and Asia."[15]

Fragment 2:
...Æschylus, in the *Prometheus Loosed*, thus speaks:
"There [is] the sacred wave, and the coralled bed of the Erythræan Sea, and [there] the luxuriant marsh of the Ethiopians, situated near the ocean, glitters like polished brass; where daily in the soft and tepid stream, the all-seeing sun bathes his undying self, and refreshes his weary steeds."[16]

Prometheus replies by telling the chorus of Titans about his sufferings and his benefits to humanity.

Fragment 3
Let us now listen to Aeschylus.... How does he make Prometheus bear the pain inflicted on him for his theft [of fire] at Lemnos ... nailed to Caucasus, he says,—
"Oh heaven-born Titans, partners of my blood,
Behold your brother bound to flinty rocks.
As timid sailors fasten ships by night
With line and anchor when the waves dash high,

---

15 The fragments are from Arrian, *Voyage in the Euxine* 99. 22. verses 194 and 184. The translation is from *Arrian's voyage round the Euxine Sea translated and accompanied with a geographical dissertation and maps*, translated by William Falconer (Oxford, J. Cooke and Caldwell and Davies, 1805) p. 15.

16 The fragment is from Strabo i. 2. 27. This translation is from *The Geography of Strabo. Literally translated, with notes, in three volumes*, translated by H. C. Hamilton and W. Falconer (London. George Bell & Sons. 1903) vol. 1, p. 27.

So has the son of Saturn nailed me here
By iron-working Vulcan's power and skill.
These spikes with cruel cunning he has driven
Through flesh and bone into the beetling cliff;
And in this camp of Furies I must dwell.
Each third day, as it dawns, with fateful wing
Jove's carrion bird fastens his talons on me,
And fiercely feeds upon my quivering entrails;
Then with my liver crammed and satiate.
With hideous shriek he takes his flight on high,
And brushes with his tail my trickling blood.
Then as my liver grows he comes again,
And fills and stuffs anew his hateful maw.
Thus feed I still this keeper of my prison,
Whose gluttony is my unceasing woe;
For, as you see, in adamantine bonds,
I cannot drive the foul bird from my breast.
So on this lonely crag I bear my torment.
Praying for death to close my term of ill.
But far from death the will of Jove repels me.
This ancient doom, through centuries of horror,
Has held me in its grasp since first the snow,
Thawed by the sun-heat on the mountain's summit.
Coursed down the rugged sides of Caucasus."[17]

Fragment 4

… Prometheus, or, in other words, the power to think and reason,

"…gives the foal of horse and ass, and get

---

[17] The fragment is from Cicero, *Tusculan Disputations* II 10. This translation is from *Cicero's Tusculan Disputations,* translated by Andrew P. Peabody (Boston, Little, Brown, and Company, 1886) p. 103. Cicero translated Aeschylus' text into Latin, and he uses the Roman names of the Greek gods: Saturn for Kronos, Jove for Zeus, and Vulcan for Hephaistus.

Of bull, to serve us, and assume our tasks,"
as Aeschylus puts it.[18]

Heracles comes to free Prometheus from his bonds. Prometheus advises Heracles about the journey that he will take to perform his twelve labors.

Fragment 5
"Go straight this way, and first of all you will come upon the northern winds, where you should beware of a rushing whirlwind, lest, twisting suddenly, it snatch you up in a stormy blast."[19]

Fragment 6
"And then you will come to a people, the most just and most hospitable of all mortals, the Gabians, where neither plough nor ground-cleaving pronged fork cuts the earth, but the self-sown lands bear sufficient nourishment for mortals."[20]

Fragment 7
Æschylus ... says,
"But the Scythians, governed by good laws, and feeding on cheese of mares' milk."[21]

---

18 This translation is from Plutarch, *Moralia*, translated by Frank Cole Babbitt (Loeb Classical Library, Cambridge, Massachusetts, Harvard University Press and London, William Heinemann Ltd, 1928) volume ii, p. 81.

19 The fragment is from Galen, *Commentary on Hippocrates' Epidemics* vi, xvii. 1. The translation was done for this edition by Marissa Anne Henry.

20 The fragment is from Stephen of Byzantium, *Lexicon* 7. 5. The translation was done for this edition by Marissa Anne Henry.

21 The fragment is from Strabo, *Geography* vii. 3. 7. The translation is from

Fragment 8
Æschylus ... makes Prometheus utter the following, whilst directing Hercules the road from the Caucasus to the Hesperides:

> "'There you will come to the undaunted army of the Ligurians, where, resistless though you be, sure am I you will not worst them in battle; for it is fated that there your darts shall fail you; nor will you be able to take up a stone from the ground, since the country consists of soft mould; but Jupiter, beholding your distress, will compassionate you, and overshadowing the earth with a cloud, he will cause it to hail round stones, which you hurling against the Ligurian army, will soon put them to flight!'"[22]

The play's climax begins with the arrival of the eagle that comes to eat Prometheus' liver. Heracles kills the eagle, and Prometheus expresses his gratitude.

Fragment 9
Hercules, having bent his bow, before he let fly at the bird which he intended to hit, invoked another Deity, as we find in Aeschylus,

> "Hunter Apollo, and to hunters kind,

The Geography of Strabo, op. cit., vol. 1, p. 462.

22 The fragment is from Strabo, *Geography* iv. 1. 7. This translation is from *The Geography of Strabo. op. cit.*, vol. 1, p. 223. Strabo describes the actual location that he thinks this quotation refers to "Between Marseilles and the outlets of the Rhone there is a circular plain, about 100 stadia distant from the sea, and about 100 stadia in diameter. It has received the name of the Stony Plain, from the circumstance of its being covered with stones the size of the fist, from beneath which an abundant herbage springs up for the pasturage of cattle."

Direct this arrow to the mark designed."[23]

Fragment 10
... the feeling which the Prometheus of Aeschylus has towards Heracles, when, having been saved by him, he says: —
"I hate the sire, but dearly love this child of his."[24]

There is an archaic black figure krater showing Heracles shooting the eagle while Prometheus is still bound.[25] Assuming that Aeschylus followed this version of the myth, Prometheus was still bound at this point in the play.

Missing Details

Two key issues that are left out of the summary above, because there are no fragments that refer to them. Why did Zeus allow Heracles to kill the eagle? Since Prometheus was bound when Heracles killed the eagle, how was Prometheus freed?

There are other accounts of the Prometheus myth that help us in these missing details.

---

23 The fragment is from Plutarch, *On Love* 14. 757E. This translation is from *Plutarch's Morals. Translated From The Greek By Several Hands. Corrected And Revised by William W. Goodwin, Ph. D., Professor Of Greek Literature In Harvard University. An Introduction By Ralph Waldo Emerson* (Boston, Little, Brown and Company. 1878) vol. 4, p. 276.

24 The fragment is from Plutarch, *Life of Pompey* 1. This translation is from Plutarch, *The Parallel Lives*, translated by Bernadotte Perrin (Cambridge, Harvard University Press, Loeb Classical Library, 1917) Vol. V, p. 117.

25 This krater is in the museum collection of the National Museum, Athens, Greece. Catalogue Number: Athens 16384. Beazley Archive Number: 320285. Attributed to Nettos Painter, c 625 - 575 BC. A krater is a large vase-like vessel used for mixing wine and water.

Killing of the Eagle

If our reconstruction of this play is correct, we know that Zeus and Prometheus were not reconciled at the time when Heracles killed the eagle, because after being saved by Heracles, Prometheus says (in fragment 10) that he still hates Zeus, the sire of Heracles.

Another account of the myth tells us that Zeus willed that Heracles kill the eagle. Hesiod, writing before Aeschylus' time, said:

> And ready-witted Prometheus he [Zeus] bound with inextricable bonds, cruel chains, and drove a shaft through his middle, and set on him a long-winged eagle, which used to eat his immortal liver; but by night the liver grew as much again everyway as the long-winged bird devoured in the whole day. That bird Heracles, the valiant son of shapely-ankled Alcmene, slew; and delivered the son of Iapetus from the cruel plague, and released him from his affliction—not without the will of Olympian Zeus who reigns on high, that the glory of Heracles the Theban-born might be yet greater than it was before over the plenteous earth. This, then, he regarded, and honoured his famous son; though he was angry, he ceased from the wrath which he had before....[26]

Pseudo-Apollodorus, writing later than Aeschylus, said in his summary of Greek myths that Heracles' aid to Prometheus was connected with the death of the centaur, Chiron. Heracles was chasing other centaurs who took refuge with Chiron, and then:

---

26 The fragment is from Hesiod, *Theogony*, verse 524 *et seq.*, This translation is from Hesiod, *Theogony*, translated by Hugh G. Evelyn-White (Cambridge, Mass., Harvard University Press, Loeb Classical Library, 1914)

As the centaurs cowered about Chiron, Hercules shot an arrow at them, which, passing through the arm of Elatus, stuck in the knee of Chiron. Distressed at this, Hercules ran up to him, drew out the shaft, and applied a medicine which Chiron gave him. But the hurt proving incurable, Chiron retired to the cave and there he wished to die, but he could not, for he was immortal. However, Prometheus offered himself to Zeus to be immortal in his stead, and so Chiron died.[27]

These accounts of the myth help us fill in the missing detail about the killing of the eagle in *Prometheus Unbound* if we compare them with something that Hermes says to Prometheus near the end of *Prometheus Bound*. If Prometheus does not reveal the prophecy, Hermes says,

> Zeus'
> Winged dog, a blood-thirsty eagle, ravenously
> Shall tear the great rag of thy body,
> Creeping an uninvited guest all day,
> And banquet on thy liver black by eating.
> Of such suffering expect not any end,
> Before some god appear
> Succeeding to thy labors, and wish to go to rayless
> Hades, and the dark depths of Tartarus.
> Therefore deliberate; since this is not made
> Boasting, but in earnest spoken;
> For to speak falsely does not know the mouth
> Of Zeus, but every word he does.

---

[27] The fragment is from Apollodorus, *The Library* 2.5.4. This translation is from Apollodorus, *The Library*, translated by Sir James George Frazer, (Cambridge, MA, Harvard University Press; London, William Heinemann Ltd., Loeb Classical Library, 1921).

Hermes seems to mean that the suffering will never end unless Prometheus reveals the prophecy because it seems impossible that a god would voluntarily give up his immortality, but apparently, these words of Zeus were fulfilled literally in *Prometheus Unbound*. Chiron was willing to give up his immortality, and there must have been a passage in the play where Heracles explained that Zeus allowed him to kill the eagle because of this sacrifice of an immortal, as Hermes had prophesied.

Freeing of Prometheus

If Prometheus was still bound when Heracles killed the eagle, then how was he freed?

Another account of this myth tells us:

> Hercules killed this vulture, but he feared to free Prometheus lest he offend his father. [28]

Judging from this fragment, the real climax of the play must come after Heracles kills the eagle, when Zeus frees Prometheus. Presumably, Hermes comes and tells Heracles that Zeus now gives him permission to unbind Prometheus.

This raises a key question to understanding the trilogy. Was Zeus forced to free Prometheus, even though they were not reconciled, to make him reveal the prophecy that Zeus will have a son who will overthrow him if he marries Thetis? Or did Zeus free Prometheus voluntarily, as he had freed the other Titans voluntarily, even though they were not yet reconciled and Prometheus had not revealed the prophecy?

The second possibility does more credit to Zeus, since it shows that he was not intimidated by Prometheus' threat

---

28 The quotation is from Maurus Servius Honoratus, *Commentary on Vergil's Bucolics*, VI, 42. The translation was done for this edition by Charles Siegel.

and was confident that, if he freed Prometheus, they would be reconciled and Prometheus would reveal the prophecy.

This second possibility is also consistent with Zeus' allowing Heracles to kill the eagle and free Prometheus from his suffering, even though Zeus and Prometheus were not reconciled.

Finally, this second possibility is consistent with Prometheus' prophesy in *Prometheus Bound* that he will not reveal the secret until after he is freed:

> ... nor ever
> Shrinking from his firm threats, will I
> Declare this, till from cruel
> Bonds he may release....

The most plausible conclusion is that *Prometheus Unbound* ended as Zeus magnanimously freed Prometheus, even though the two were not yet reconciled and even though Prometheus had not yet revealed the prophesy about Thetis.

Prometheus the Fire Bearer
Description and Fragments

If our reconstruction of *Prometheus Unbound* is correct and Prometheus was not reconciled with Zeus in this play, then the subject of *Prometheus the Fire Bearer* must be their reconciliation and Prometheus' acceptance of his place in the new divine order under the reign of Zeus.

As part of this reconciliation, Prometheus reveals the prophesy that, if Thetis bears Zeus' child, the child will overthrow Zeus. Perhaps there is also a prophesy that, instead of Zeus, Thetis will wed Peleus and bear their child Achilles.

Aeschylus' account of how Prometheus accepts his place in the new order would provide an origin myth about the founding of the Athenian festival *Prometheia* and the altar of Prometheus in the Academy. As Wecklein says in the introduction:

> Just outside of Athens was the *Kolonos hippos*, a hill sacred to Poseidon, which furnished the potters' quarter of the city, the *Kerameikos*, with admirable clay for the famous and much-sought Attic vases. Between this hill and the city lay the Academy, the sacred grove of the hero Academus. Here Prometheus was worshipped in conjunction with Hephaestus and Athena. In the space dedicated

to the goddess Athena stood an old statue of Prometheus, with an altar. At the entrance was a pedestal with a relief representing Prometheus and Hephaestus. Prometheus was here figured as the more prominent and older god, with a sceptre in his hand; Hephaestus as younger and less important. On the same pedestal a common altar of the two deities was represented. In honor of Prometheus the festival called *Prometheia* was annually celebrated, with a torch-race from the Academy to the city. The torches were lighted at the altar of Prometheus, and the runners endeavored to outstrip each other without extinguishing their torches.

This is how Prometheus was honored in Athens, as part of a religion that had Zeus at the top of the divine hierarchy, so the ceremony is an apt symbol of the reconciliation of the two and of Prometheus' acceptance of his place in the new order.

The establishment of the altar would also be a fitting conclusion to the trilogy, because it shows Prometheus as more important than Hephaestus—a strong contrast with the beginning of the trilogy, where Hephaestus is binding Prometheus.

Surviving Fragments

The few surviving fragments of *Prometheus the Fire Bearer* do not help us understand the play.

Many sources list only one fragment:

Fragment 1
... in the Fire-bringing Prometheus of Aeschylus ... it runs thus:

"When proper, keeping silent, and saying what is fit."[29]

There is also a scholium (an ancient note written in the margin of a manuscript) in a manuscript of *Prometheus Bound* that says Prometheus said in *Prometheus the Fire Bearer* that his punishment was to be bound for

Fragment 2
"thrice ten thousand years."[30]

Both these fragments tell us virtually nothing about the action of the play.

There is another quotation that might tell us something about this play but is problematic. Athenaeus wrote:

Fragment 3
Aeschylus also, in his *Prometheus Unbound*, says distinctly—
"And therefore we, in honour of Prometheus,
Place garlands on our heads, a poor atonement
For the sad chains with which his limbs were bound."[31]

---

29 The fragment is from Aulus Cornelius Gellius, *Noctes Atticae* (Attic Nights) xiii, 19. The translation is from *The Attic Nights of Aulus Gellius*, translated by J. C. Rolfe (London, William Heinemann and New York, G.P. Putnam, Loeb Classical Library, 1927), Vol. II, p. 461.

30 This term of 30,000 years is puzzling, because Prometheus was freed in much less time than this. Aeschylus has him predict in *Prometheus Bound* that he will be freed by Io's descendent in the thirteenth generation, and this prediction is fulfilled when Heracles frees him in *Prometheus Unbound*. Thirteen generations is about 400 years.

31 The fragment is from Athenaeus, *Deipnosophists or Banquet of the*

This fragment has been attributed to all three of the Prometheus plays.

Some scholars, including Mark Griffith, believe that this fragment shows that *Prometheus Unbound* included the reconciliation between Prometheus and Zeus and the establishment of the *Prometheia*, the festival when the Athenians wore garlands on their heads. For this reason, Griffith believes that the action of the trilogy is completed in *Prometheus Unbound* and that *Prometheus the Fire Bearer* must be the first play of the trilogy. This seems unlikely, because *Prometheus Unbound* gives much more background about the dispute between Prometheus and Zeus than would be needed if *Prometheus the Fire Bearer* came before it and provided this background, as many scholars, including Sommerstein,[32] have said.

Some scholars claim this fragment means that Prometheus prophesied in *Prometheus Unbound* that this honor would result from his reconciliation with Zeus in *Prometheus the Fire Bearer*.

Some scholars believe that Athanaeus got the reference wrong and Aeschylus actually said this in *Prometheus the Fire Bearer*.

Learned: Literally Translated by C.D. Yonge XV: 16 (London, Henry Bohn, 1854) p. 1076.

---

32 Aeschylus, *Fragments*, ed. Sommerstein, p. 212. Sommerstein also claims that *Prometheus the Fire Bearer* could not possibly have come after *Prometheus Unbound*, because the action is completely finished in *Prometheus Unbound*. Because he believes that *Prometheus the Fire Bearer* could not have come before or after *Prometheus Bound*, he concludes that *Prometheus the Fire Bearer* must be another name for the satyr play *Prometheus the Fire Kindler*, and he combines the fragments from the two. This view implies that there were two Prometheus tragedies rather than a trilogy, and Sommerstein suggests that the Prometheus tragedies were not by Aeschylus and were written for a city that produced sets of two plays rather than trilogies.

Either of the last two suggestions seems plausible, and in either case, this fragment would show that *Prometheus the Fire Bearer* is about the reconciliation between Prometheus and Zeus and the establishment of the *Prometheia*.

The Trilogy

Thus, the most plausible reconstruction of the Prometheus trilogy is the following:

In *Prometheus Bound*, Zeus has recently become ruler of the gods and is solidifying his rule using violence. He wanted to destroy humans, and when Prometheus saved them, Zeus punished him by chaining him to a mountain. When Io passes by, Prometheus predicts her wanderings, predicts that her descendent will free him, and predicts that Zeus will have a son who will dethrone him. He refuses to tell Hermes which woman will bear this son, so Zeus has an eagle eat his liver repeatedly to compel him to reveal this secret. Hermes predicts that he will not be freed until he tells the secret or until a god gives up his immortality, something that it seems will never happen.

In *Prometheus Unbound*, generations later, Io's descendent Heracles passes by. Prometheus predicts his twelve labors. Heracles kills the eagle that is eating Prometheus' liver but will not free him without permission from Zeus. Somehow, we learn that that Chiron has given up his immortality and Zeus has given permission; probably Hermes comes and announces this. The play ends as Heracles frees Prometheus, though he has not reconciled with Zeus.

In *Prometheus the Fire Bearer*, Prometheus reconciles with Zeus, tells Zeus that he can avoid being dethroned by not having a child with Thetis, and accepts his place under Zeus in the new order, explaining the origin of the Athenian *Prometheia*.

Zeus' character changes dramatically in the first two plays. *Prometheus Bound* occurs early in his reign, when he is trying to establish his authority though brute force, and he tortures Prometheus to try to learn which woman would bear the child who would dethrone him. *Prometheus Unbound* occurs later, when his authority is well established and he is confident enough to free Prometheus without learning about the child first. This magnanimous gesture convinces Prometheus to tell him who would bear the child who would overthrow him and to accept his place in the new divine order headed by Zeus, where he is honored during the *Prometheia*.

Our understanding of *Prometheus Bound* is based on the one play where Zeus is a violent tyrant and Prometheus refuses to obey him. Romantics, such as Shelley, admired Prometheus as a rebel who resisted unjust authority.

But when we look at the entire trilogy, we can see that the relationship between Zeus and Prometheus is more complex. Zeus becomes more humane, so Prometheus is willing to accept his place in the new order ruled by Zeus. The trilogy is about the establishment of the classical order, not about romantic rebellion.

A comparison with Aeschylus' *Oresteia*, the one complete trilogy that survives, confirms this view of the Prometheus trilogy.

In the first play, *Agamemnon*, Clytemnestra kills her husband Agamemnon when he returns from the Trojan War.

In the second play, *Libation Bearers*, Agamemnon's

son, Orestes, avenges his father's murder by killing his mother, but as the play ends, he finds he is pursued by the Eumenides (or Furies), who take revenge on those who kill their parents.

In the third play, *The Eumenides*, Orestes flees, pursued by the Eumenides, and finally reaches Athens, where he throws himself at the foot of a statue of Athena. Athena creates a jury to try his crime; ultimately, the jury's vote is tied, which leads to Orestes being acquitted. Athena convinces the Eumenides to accept the verdict and brings them to their new shrine, at the foot of the Areopagus. The ancient goddeses accept this place in the new divine order, where they will be honored by the citizens of Athens.

The Areopagus was originally a council of elders held on the Hill of Ares and was an important part of the Athenian government, but in Aeschylus' time, it had lost its traditional powers and continued to function as a final court of appeals in murder trials.

Thus, the final play of the *Oresteia* trilogy explains the origins of Athenian institutions of Aeschylus' day: the function of the Areopagus as the court of appeals in murder trials, and the shrine to the Eumenides at the foot of the Areopagus.

The end of *Prometheus Unbound* is reminiscent of the end of *Libation Bearers*. In *Libation Bearers*, the tension of the first two plays of the trilogy is resolved when Orestes kills his mother, but a new tension is introduced when the Eumenides appear, which will be resolved in the last play of the trilogy when the Eumenides accept their place in the new divine order. Likewise, in *Prometheus Unbound*, the tension of the first two plays is resolved when Prometheus is freed, but a new tension is introduced when Prometheus says he hates Zeus. This new tension is resolved in the last play of the trilogy, as Prometheus and Zeus are reconciled and Prometheus accepts his place in the new divine order, where he will be honored by the citizens of Athens.

Made in United States
Troutdale, OR
10/12/2023

13623405R00061